TO UNDERSTAND
AND BE
UNDERSTOOD

Erik Blumenthal Dip. Psych. (born in 1914) is a prac-
tising psychotherapist and analyst. He is a lecturer at
the Alfred Adler Institute in Zürich, President of the
Swiss Society for Individual Psychology, and Director
of the International Committee for Adlerian Summer
Schools and Institutes. He has written a number of
books on child-rearing, self-education, marriage and
old age, and is married with six children and nine
grandchildren.

TO UNDERSTAND
AND BE
UNDERSTOOD

A Practical Guide to Successful Relationships

Erik Blumenthal

DEDICATION

This book is dedicated to all people
who have recognised the senselessness of strife, struggle and force;
who are tired of conflict, confrontation and aggression;
who wish to learn to live in peace with their partner, their family,
the different generations, with friends, colleagues, acquaintances,
relatives and neighbours, with those of other nations, other races
and other religions, and not least with themselves.

TO UNDERSTAND AND BE UNDERSTOOD

Oneworld Publications Ltd
1c Standbrook House, Old Bond Street, London W1X 3TD
PO Box 1908, Limassol, Cyprus

Originally published in German under the title
Verstehen und verstanden werden © Rex-Verlag München/Lużern 1977
This English edition © Oneworld Publications 1987
All rights reserved. Copyright under Berne Convention

Reprinted 1987

British Library Cataloguing in Publication Data
Blumenthal, Erik
To understand and be understood:
a practical guide to successful relationships
1. Interpersonal relations
I. Title
158'.2   HM132

ISBN 1-85168-004-7

Printed and bound in Great Britain by
The Guernsey Press Co. Ltd, Guernsey, Channel Islands.

Translated by Nancy Benvenga

CONTENTS

FOREWORD

More and more people are beginning to realise that all is not well with the way in which we relate to each other. They are experiencing difficulties in their family relationships, in their closest friendships, and with their wider circle of acquaintances, both in their private and working lives.

Apart from a few mentally or emotionally disturbed people, scarcely a human being exists who lives a completely solitary life. Even in large cities, people who live alone have some contact with others on a regular basis, while most of us have extensive experience of social relationships.

Why then does this experience serve us so poorly? Why has the social historian Arnold Toynbee been able to say that while we have developed dramatically in intellectual, scientific and technical spheres, our level of human relationship is much what it was five thousand years ago? People loved and hated in ancient Babylon much as they do today.

Although it appears that human beings have developed lopsidedly in this way, at the same time we have also developed the sciences which could assist us in our social relationships: psychology, sociology, politics and economics. And how does religion come into the picture, that important resource which, in all its various forms, includes among its concerns many rules and principles for social conduct. Every major religion teaches about the love of God and love for our fellow man, and love is undoubtedly a fundamental ingredient in successful relationships.

What prevents us putting this knowledge into practice? To me there seems to be only one answer: our prejudices, and we can only overcome these through a new understanding, an understanding of ourselves and of others.

This book is concerned with understanding each other; I discussed means of gaining greater understanding of ourselves in my previous book, *The Way to Inner Freedom*.[1] Both books are based on my experience with thousands of people, both in groups, seminars, courses and lectures, and in my psychotherapy practice. The examples in this book have come from these encounters, many of which have, for obvious reasons, been modified. They are examples not of people who are mentally ill, but of everyday experiences we can all identify with.

The chapter headings present those principles which I consider to be most important in learning to interrelate effectively. The quotations at the beginning of the chapters come from religious sources, demonstrating the fundamental unity of religion and science.

I am indebted to Alfred Adler's teachings on individual psychology, my teacher Dr Alexander Mueller, and my friend Prof. Dr Rudolf Driekurs. I thank my beloved wife for her knowledge, love and faith, and my son Stefan for the many valuable suggestions he made while reading the manuscript.

Erik Blumenthal
Immenstaad, Germany

1

DECIDE MORE CONSCIOUSLY

'All that which ye potentially possess can be manifested only as a result of your own volition.'[2]

It is Mrs Martin's birthday. Her sister and mother have come to visit. Mr Martin, probably for no other reason than to get the conversation going, innocently tells them how he ordered his wife's present four weeks ago. It still hasn't arrived, he says, so he had nothing to give her this morning.

'Typical!' is the mother's reaction, and she asks him whether he had at least given her a card — to her such things are extremely important. Mr Martin grew up in a family in which the routine giving of cards was not so important, and when he says that he hasn't, the mother cannot restrain herself from letting everyone know that she would have expected nothing else from a man like that. Within a very short space of time the atmosphere has become so dreadful that the mother leaves early, completely spoiling Mrs Martin's birthday, and leaving her sad and tearful.

And so it goes on. A forceful mother has apparently been able to manipulate her grown child's emotional state. How is it possible for a person to be so deeply influenced by another? Everyone who gets angry, frustrated or unhappy, generally knows exactly whose fault it is. We are accustomed to blaming other people for our negative feelings and our emotional states.

Most people are unaware of the possibility of any other reaction, but there is an alternative, which follows from the realisation that no one in the world can make me angry, because my anger is my anger and nobody else's. Only I can invoke my anger, and I can choose whether or not to express it. When somebody else gets angry, they too — though often unconsciously — have chosen to get angry. We are all decision-making human beings who decide on some level to do everything we do. Each thought, each feeling, each desire, each expectation and each expression is the result of a decision, for the most part made subconsciously.

Most people do not want to accept this realisation, because they do not want to take the responsibility for their bad feelings. It seems so much more rewarding to blame others. This way we always have a wonderful excuse for our bad temper and moodiness: 'It's your fault!'

In our example, everyone thinks the mother is to blame. Yet Mrs Martin, the birthday girl, could have decided not to react angrily to her mother's aggression. She could also have decided to feel sorry for her mother and help her. At the same time, it would have been important to cast a loving glance at her husband, or even to have given him a hug. That would have shown that she did not mind the delay in receiving the present. If the two of them, husband and wife, had shown their love and unanimity in this way, the mother's aggression would merely have been a ripple in the ocean, and she in turn would have learned how well 'the children' loved and understood each other, so that such small mishaps were of no importance.

The next conscious step that Mrs Martin could have taken might have been to consider *how* she could help her mother, because when her mother behaves in this way it shows how unhappy she really is. Aggressive people are usually expressing anger arising from hurtful experiences they have had, often as children. They learn to use their aggression to excuse their own faults, to demand attention, to feel superior (or at least to avoid a sense of inferiority), or to avenge themselves for an injustice which they feel has been done to them. Thoughts like this may not have occurred to Mrs Martin, but adopting this sort of approach would have prevented her from reacting impulsively to her mother's behaviour.

Perhaps you are thinking that you would have to be superhuman to have such an attitude — only saints could behave this way! But you do not need to be a fanatical perfectionist to make these suggestions work, just an optimistic realist. The following reflections may help to clarify the method of deciding more consciously.

The mother had no right to ruin her daughter's birthday. Mr and Mrs Martin have been treated unjustly, yet they have done nothing wrong. So who is better off, the person who has done wrong or the person to whom the wrong has been done? Mr and Mrs Martin are happy; they love each other. Why should they suffer the injustice the mother inflicts on them? They can recognise that people who spread poison and want to make others unhappy cannot be happy themselves, and therefore need help.

Of course, Mr and Mrs Martin could misuse this awareness, and help the mother simply in order to feel superior. There is nothing that a person cannot misuse, and purity of motive will be looked at in the next chapter.

A change of thinking is required in order to recognise that it is not other people who make us angry. We ourselves determine our feelings and moods, even if it is subconscious. This realisation leads to another, which is equally important. We have a vested interest, even if we are not

11

always aware of it, in choosing to have feelings which have a disruptive effect on our relationships.

2

DECIDE FOR PURER MOTIVES

*'The third virtue of humanity is the goodwill
which is the basis of good actions'*[3]

Human beings, however they relate to other people, pursue
purposes, intentions and ambitions of which they are not
necessarily conscious.

Excuse

Rita lives in a university town in a furnished room. The
family who have rented her the room are very noisy, so her
studies are constantly being disturbed, which makes her
irritable and angry.

Rita has lived there for months, but until now has kept her
anger to herself, and has not considered looking for another
room. Although she knows that she feels angry, she does not
understand that she has deliberately chosen to keep her
anger inactive because it provides her with the perfect excuse
should she fail in her studies. She has little faith in herself,
and lives in continuous fear of failure — hence her
investment in her anger. If she were aware of this
investment, she could learn to take less notice of the noise, or
even to ignore it. She might even decide to take some decisive
action — to talk to the family or find another room.

Attention

Mr Miller comes home from work in a bad mood. His wife greets him lovingly as usual. Noticing how angry he is, she asks him what has happened at the office. He tells her how recently his colleagues have seemed to take less notice of him; then today, when he asked a perfectly straight-forward question, they virtually ignored him. His wife gives him a hug and comforts him. Together they discuss what he could do to improve the situation. After the conversation, Mr Miller's bad mood has disappeared.

This example shows clearly that the purpose of the bad mood, the motive for it, was to obtain sympathy and attention. This may sound improbable, but remember that this sort of motive often operates quite unconsciously.

Superiority

Mrs Cook is clearing the table. A knife falls on the floor, and her husband reacts immediately: 'You can't even clear the table without dropping something!' Mrs Cook feels so angry that she turns round and shouts at her husband, defending herself loudly. She feels unfairly treated, and reacts just as a child would. If the situation had been reversed she would have acted quite differently. Mr Cook reacts to her anger with increased aggression, and as usual, they provoke each other until a big quarrel develops and one of them leaves the room.

This sort of situation is an archetypal power struggle. Mr Cook lacks self-confidence, so he considers it necessary — again unconsciously of course — to disparage his wife. When he tells her how stupid she is, he means that he considers himself to be cleverer than her, and thereby surreptitiously achieves for himself a feeling of superiority over his wife. He needs this feeling to make himself feel important.

How could Mrs Cook have behaved differently to her

husband's insult? If she had understood the reason behind his need to disparage her she might have seen, beneath the surface of this grown man, the hurt child who felt he had to disparage others in order not to appear inferior. She only makes a small mistake, while he makes a big one. He abuses her slight mishap, making a mountain out of a molehill. Instead of feeling humiliated and being lured into her husband's game, she could have looked at ways in which she could help him, either by choosing not to react at all, or by passing over the incident with a little joke.

Retaliation

Mrs Cutter has just moved to a small town, and goes into a shop in which she is not yet known. She waits to be served, but just as her turn comes the clock strikes one, and a crowd of workers from a nearby firm come in to buy their lunchtime sandwiches. The assistant tells her that she must serve these people next, or they will not get their lunch. Mrs Cutter protests, but the assistant is unmoved. Mrs Cutter storms out: 'I'll buy what I need somewhere else!' she hisses.

Mrs Cutter is taking her revenge on the shop assistant. The purpose of her anger is retaliation. Her anger is justifiable, but what does she achieve with it? Perhaps the assistant feels angry too; the workers presumably seem important. But it is Mrs Cutter who suffers most from her anger — she has to find another shop, which takes time and effort.

What could she have done? If she had already known how to avoid anger she might have prevailed upon the assistant, or turned to the workers and explained that her husband would soon be back from work and would have to wait for his lunch — they would surely have understood this. She could have let the workers go ahead and been patient and good-humoured for five minutes. Those five minutes, occupied in pleasant conversation, could have enriched everyone present.

These examples illustrate some of the motives behind our social behaviour of which we may be completely or partly unaware. As Adler says, 'man knows more than he understands.' But the most interesting thing is that where socially disturbing behaviour is concerned, these four motives — excuse, attention, superiority and retaliation — can explain our anger (though there is also a range of secondary goals).

We reach these motives not by asking '*Why* am I getting angry?' or '*Why* is the other person getting angry?', but by asking instead 'What is the purpose of the anger?'. The question 'Why?' is justified in the realm of the physical and material, but where mental or emotional matters are involved the causative way of looking at things is generally of secondary concern — it is ineffective, it improves and achieves nothing. The answer may be interesting, but it usually only offers a seemingly plausible explanation for something which has a deeper purpose. In emotional matters it is more instructive to proceed 'teleologically' — to recognise the purpose, the goal, the intention, the meaning or the motive of a way of behaving.

A knowledge of the four motives of excuse, attention, superiority and retaliation not only increases our understanding of each other, but can lead, often in unsuspected ways, to more harmonious, positive and peaceful relationships. Such an understanding helps us to see how we can proceed when we feel angry:

1) I can recognise the goal I am pursuing in being angry.
2) I will thereby understand the other person better.
3) My attitude towards them will thus change.
4) Once I have explained their motive to them in an appropriate way, they cannot continue as before.

To see clearly how this method works, let us take another example.

Mr and Mrs Potter are out walking, and meet one of Mrs Potter's friends. The two women arrange a time to meet. 'Make a note of it,' says Mr Potter. 'No,' says Mrs Potter, 'I can remember.' When she and her friend arrange a further meeting, however, she does decide to write it down. 'It's always the same,' says her husband, 'you never do what I suggest first time round!' The banter continues for a while until they both realise that Mrs Potter's friend is waiting for them to stop.

Although this is clearly another power struggle, and not even a concealed one, neither of the participants has really recognised it as such, a very common occurrence in our everyday relationships.

In this example the husband is the more aggressive person, and Mrs Potter, being for the moment the one being attacked, is in a better position to behave appropriately. Taking our four 'steps of understanding', she could have looked at it this way:

1) In order to understand her husband's socially disturbing behaviour, she could ask herself 'How am I reacting?' and 'How does he react to my reaction?'

She defends herself against her husband's I-know-better attitude, therefore she is not seeking an excuse. Neither does she need to attract attention — she already has it. She is hardly looking for revenge, and so only the goal of superiority remains. Is that what she really wants? Not directly, but she does want to avoid the position of inferiority in which her husband wants to place her. In the ensuing power struggle it is superiority that is at stake.

2) By recognising the goal, Mrs Potter understands her husband better. But as long as somebody finds it necessary to demonstrate superiority, they betray their

17

fear of being inferior.

3) When Mrs Potter recognises this, she can change her attitude towards her husband, and can see the little boy against whom she hardly needs to defend herself. It is he who needs help. She can recognise that the present situation is about *his* problem, which she does not need to make *hers*.

4) The first step towards helping him is not to be drawn into an argument, because her husband cannot argue on his own. A soldier alone on the battlefield has no one to fight. Also, by recognising her husband's true motive, she cannot be made angry by him; thus she can remain calm and even-tempered. She can now decide to behave lovingly towards her husband, and even to give him the power that he wants. She does not have to be powerless or inferior in order to offer him power. Other practical measures are discussed in later chapters.

This method of recognising one of the four immediate goals should be used not only with other people, but with yourself too. No one readily admits that they are pursuing a negative goal, which makes the application of the method to yourself quite an exercise in self-awareness! I say more about this method of self-awareness in my book on self-education[4].

3

BELIEVE MORE STRONGLY

'As ye have faith, so shall your powers and blessings be'[5]

Five outer and five inner senses

We are not only beings with bodies, and not only beings that also have minds — in addition to physical and mental powers we also have spiritual powers. The physical powers are familiar to us: they are our most primitive powers, powers which we have in common with all the animals — the five outer senses of perception. When people resort to physical means of expression, to brute force, at that instant they have left the level worthy of human beings and put themselves at the level of the animals.

Among the mental powers are the five inner senses. The first inner sense is the common sense which mediates between the inner and outer senses. It conveys that which has been perceived by the five outer senses on to the second inner sense — the power of imagination. After we have imagined whatever has been perceived, we reflect on it using our reasoning, form it into concepts, then convey what has been conceptualised to our fifth inner sense, our memory.

Our spiritual powers include intuition, and the power of expectancy or faith. Unfortunately these spiritual powers are not taken seriously enough nowadays because they elude scientific research, research which works predominantly with the techniques of scientific method. The spiritual dimension is independent of the categories of space and time, and cannot be comprehended by measuring, counting and weighing.

Some years ago I was invited to speak at a university, and talked there about the power of faith, by which I meant not only religious faith, but part of the spiritual dimension of being human[6]. After the lecture, the professor who had invited me asked whether it would not be better to avoid the word 'faith', since it would be sure to evoke prejudice in many people through its religious association. Surely, he said, it would be better to use the word 'anticipation', since psychology already acknowledges the power of expectation. Would it not be better to talk about the power of anticipation? Well, he is right that this sounds more scientific, but can we not reinstate the word 'faith'? It has been used by many wise people over the centuries, who have acknowledged that there is no greater power in human life than the power of faith, the power of expectancy, the power of anticipation:

'All things are possible to them that believe.' (St Mark)

'And all that you ask in prayer, if you believe, will be granted to you.' (St Matthew)

'The first sign of faith is love.' ('Abdu'l-Bahá)

'By faith is meant, first, conscious knowledge, and second, the practice of good deeds.' ('Abdu'l-Bahá)

'All epochs which are ruled by belief . . . are brilliant, heart-stirring and fruitful for their own and future generations. All epochs, on the other hand, in which unbelief claims a miserable victory, disappear before posterity, because no one wants to be tormented with the recognition of the fruitless.' (Goethe)

'Everything wavers when faith is lacking.' (Schiller)

20

'Words are dead; faith brings life.' (Schiller)

'If you believed more in life, you would embrace more readily the moment at hand' (Nietzsche)

'Knowledge knows nothing; only faith knows.' (Rückert)

'Faith is a completely new sense, surpassing the other five.' (Luther)

'To be able to believe is the greatest power.' (Nicholas von Cues)

'Man begins sentiently, then he thinks, finally he believes.' (Börne)

A mother in a parents' group complained that her little daughter came to her bed every night and disturbed her sleep. She was advised not to let herself be disturbed by paying no attention at all to her daughter during the night, and acting as if she did not exist. She agreed to do this, and had faith that this new tactic would improve things for her and her daughter. When she awoke the next morning, she could not remember whether or not her daughter had come in during the night. Nor did she ever find out, but from that time on her daughter never again disturbed her during the night.

In purely scientific terms it is 'unbelievable' that the mother's faith could work. She did not speak to her daughter when she came home from the parents' group because she was already asleep. Yet the daughter must have sensed her mother's faith and determination. Somehow the daughter 'knew' that her nightly attempts to gain attention would no longer have any effect. We know far more than we understand.

A married woman in a psychotherapeutic group led an outwardly peaceful married life. She simply left it to her husband to make all the necessary decisions; to him she was 'only a wife'. He regarded her interest in psychology with benevolent condescension. At one of the group's meetings she announced that she would not be able to come next time. She was going away on holiday with her husband for a week, and she was sure that he would not want to return home one day earlier to enable her to participate in the group. The group asked her whether she had any say in the matter. Would she not like to become an equal partner with him in making the decision? This would be an opportunity for him, too. She understood, and decided to come to the next meeting, whatever happened.

When she got home she told her husband that she wanted to take part in the next group meeting, which would mean shortening the holiday by one day. He did not answer, but she was determined to get to the group. During the holiday they never mentioned the departure date, but one day before they had originally planned to leave — the day she had determined to go home alone on the train if necessary — her husband, to her great amazement, said: 'Darling, we'll go home tomorrow so you can get to your group.'

He had sensed her determination, which was based upon a new belief in herself.

A married couple with children were very interested in healthy and sensible nourishment for their family, and placed a great importance on eating fresh vegetables and salad. One day, however, their youngest daughter refused to eat salad. The parents were understanding enough to recognise that nothing could be achieved by force, so did not bother too much about it. They also suspected that they had overemphasised the eating of salad. They just had confidence that when it was ready the child's body would ask for fresh food again of its own accord. Their patience was tested for a long while, but they never gave up believing in healthy nutrition. It was over a year before the little girl asked for salad again, but since then she has always eaten plenty of salad.

Without their faith the parents would surely have used all the usual methods, whether good or bad, to get their child to eat healthy foods again. 'We've tried everything!' would have been their lament. But the consequences would have been that meals would have become times of constant friction, a power struggle which would inevitably have resulted in the daughter becoming an unhealthy eater.

After a two-year stay in Athens, the Hill family was returning to England. Mr Hill returned by car with the two older children, while Mrs Hill was to return by plane with their daughter, who had been born a few weeks earlier. It was Mrs Hill's job to sell the furniture. To help her, Mr Hill had drawn up a list of what the furniture had cost when it was new.

Mrs Hill did not have much faith in her business acumen, but when she arrived back in England she was able to report that she had been able to sell everything for much what she had expected. All, that is, except for the clothes cupboard — everybody had thought it was much too dear, and eventually she had only been able to get rid of it for 3,000 drachmas.

Her husband looked at her, then at the list, and burst out laughing. The cupboard had been used for two years and the mirror was cracked — and it had only cost 2,400 drachmas when it was new. He had written the '2' rather illegibly so his wife had read a '5'. It was in the firm belief that it had cost 5,400 drachmas that she had been able to get as much as 3,000, even from the usually enterprising Greeks.[7]

Whether we are conscious of it or not, we all make use of the power of faith, the greatest power in human life, every day, from morning to evening. It is not only a matter of religious faith, of belief in a spiritual principle we generally call God, but also of belief in ourselves, which we call self-confidence, and belief in others, to which we may give the label 'social concern'. It involves believing in nature, in life, in reality, in creation, and in human nature. We cannot bring up children if we do not believe in them. We cannot encourage children if we do not believe in them just as they are, just as they stand before us with all their faults, and not as they might be.[8]

Nobody would be reading this book if they did not think they could get something useful from it. Nobody would get up in the morning or go to work if they did not think it was right and sensible to do so. It matters little whether the object of the faith is the job itself, or what it represents, or the means of making the money we need.

Even in its negative manifestations we can see the colossal power of faith — in anxiety. Anxiety is the belief that something is failing, that something is going wrong, that something unpleasant is happening. It is not difficult to recognise that anxiety — lack of faith — plagues not only individual people, but the whole of contemporary humanity.

Once we have recognised the power of faith, then we can learn to train it. We can decide to believe more and more in whatever appears to us to be worthwhile, whether it is our own existence, other people and the way we relate to them, or God. Bahá'u'lláh has said: 'The faith of no man can be conditioned by anyone except himself.'[9]

In any case, it must be remembered that faith is an attribute of being human, just like feeling and thinking but on a spiritual level.

4

ACT, DO NOT REACT

*'It is actions that speak to the world and are
the cause of the progress of humanity'*[10]

There was poor cooperation where Miss Abele worked.
Everyone was dissatisfied and complained, but no one
did anything to improve the situation. People worked in
different groups, so they were never all there at the same
time. Miss Abele thought it would be a good idea if
everyone were to get together and discuss the situation,
so she asked around to see what the others thought about
having a meeting. Many of them were in favour, but
nobody did anything about arranging it. She talked to
her department head, who was also supportive of the
idea, but still nothing happened.

A few days later a colleague told her that the department head had suggested that Miss Abele had only
spoken out in order to feel important. She felt insulted,
because this had not been her intention at all, and she
had not wanted to appear superior. No discussion had yet
taken place, and she felt completely misunderstood.
None of her colleagues supported her, so she felt disappointed and even thought of resigning.

In this situation Miss Abele behaved correctly at the

beginning. She saw that something needed to happen and did something about it — she acted. Later, however, she lost her courage, because she paid too much attention to what other people said or thought — she overreacted.

Sometimes situations arise in which it would be impolite not to react, but even then we can make an action out of our reaction. We can consciously decide what to do, and remain free and independent. In this way we can control circumstances and remain masters of the situation, regardless of how difficult it is, and how we and our behaviour may appear at the time.

Miss Abele made herself so dependent upon other people's opinions because she believed too little in herself (remember Chapter 3). She felt that she needed to appear 'good' in the eyes of others, yet not put herself 'above' them. In order to avoid seeing the subjectivity and self-centredness of this attitude she decided (see Chapter 1) to feel insulted. This feeling made it possible to see the others as being unjust, and thus — but only inwardly — to disparage them, and secretly to secure for herself the feeling of superiority (Chapter 2, goal 3).

Miss Abele has not only reacted towards the others, but she has also reacted to the reactions she expected from them to her own behaviour. Had she summoned up the courage to act, to do something, she might have suggested a time and place for a meeting, having first talked to everybody concerned, without thinking in a subjective way about how other people were reacting, or whether her initiative was succeeding. She would then have felt, 'I have done what I could.' Whether the meeting had succeeded or failed there would still have been the potential for deciding what should be done next. As the saying goes: 'God give me the courage to change what I can change, the patience to bear what I cannot change, and the wisdom to distinguish the one from the other.'

On the bus on his way to work each morning, Nick, a handsome young man of nineteen, sees a young woman to whom he is very much attracted. She has a pretty face and a good figure, and he likes the gracefulness of her movements and the expression on her face. Without showing off at all, she is friendly to everyone around her, and she wears very attractive clothes. In short, everything about her seems perfect. He imagines speaking to her, but cannot pluck up the courage. The seat next to her has been free several times, but how would he begin a conversation? He would have nothing to say. She would think he was stupid. And what would the other passengers think? He knows that his friends manage to do it, but he also knows that some of their boasts and sneers have more to do with insecurity than with truth. So, feeling anxious, he always sits somewhere else.

Whatever is done or not done out of fear must be paid for. Many philosophers and psychologists have strange ideas about fear. True, very few of us are completely without fear, but fear is not a necessary part of being human. To be afraid is to have made a decision, very often in early childhood. Fear is a reaction. Every small child is frightened of things that are strange or unknown — sudden noises, for example — but it is because of the inappropriate reaction of adults to this natural childish fright that a child first decides to be afraid, since he or she soon discovers that being afraid has certain advantages, like the ability to attract attention.

Nick found a solution to his problem. An older friend of the family convinced him that young men and women do not differ greatly in their desire to find a partner, and encounters between the sexes are not only right and normal, but an essential part of being human. Nick was particularly helped by the understanding that women should not be seen as sex objects: women are physically different from men, but emotionally and spiritually they have exactly the same sort of feelings, thoughts, desires, interests and expectations. Why should this girl not have noticed him too, and why should she not want to make his acquaintance just as much as he wanted to make hers?

What might happen to him? At the very worst she could tell him that she was not interested in him — that is her right. Would this make his world fall apart?

He was able to accept all this, understand that loving — within the limits which society must set — is good and right, and see that it is more important to love than to be loved. At the next opportunity, he sat next to her on the bus.

He acted without regard to her reaction, to the reactions of others, or to his own inner reactions. Today the two of them are a happy couple.

Graham is seventeen, and is serving an apprenticeship. The foreman constantly tells Graham how useless he is, and is always shouting at him. As far as he is concerned, Graham can do nothing right. Graham tries hard, but he gets no joy or interest from his work. He would like to leave, but the thought of what his parents would say keeps him there.

It never pays to run away from anything. The feeling of failure remains, even though you might think that other people are to blame. Graham's situation is not easy, because the foreman is trying hard to render him powerless. Yet he could learn to react less. What is essential is that he learns something from the situation, and does not allow himself to be deflected from his goal by anything, including the aggressive foreman. It might help if he can keep the following thoughts in mind:

28

1) He must decide to react in new ways; if he continues react in the same way, he will remain trapped.
2) To act rather than react means: 'I want to learn.'
3) To act means to give of your best.
4) The apprenticeship is only for a limited time.
5) To deal with the situation and complete the apprenticeship would increase his courage and self-confidence.
6) He must understand that he would not naturally allow himself to be treated unworthily.
7) He can try to understand why the foreman behaves so aggressively — he might then even be able to help him (this last point is discussed in Chapter 7).

When we learn to *react* less and *act* more, we also become less impulsive, and stop letting ourselves be carried away by thoughtless emotional behaviour which can only be destructive. Impulsiveness, however, should not be confused with spontancity, which is good and creative. Spontaneous action means to act of our own accord because we have consciously decided, chosen to do so. Spontaneity springs from inner freedom; impulsiveness is a sign of our dependence.

5

LOOK BENEATH THE SURFACE

'Ultimately all the battle of life
is within the individual'[11]

Mr Thomas and the children enjoy watching television every evening. Mrs Thomas frequently gets angry about this and tries to interrupt them, either by asking the children to do the chores just as they are settling down, by producing meals during the most interesting programmes, by doing the hoovering, or by wanting to tell the family all about her problems while they watch. A favourite ploy is to sit and watch with them for a while, then complain about the poor quality of the programme and lament all the things that could have been done if they hadn't watched it.

The result is a series of accusations, recriminations and quarrels. Trouble is brewing in the household, and superficially it would appear that it is Mrs Thomas who is disturbing the peace and annoying her family. Her husband and children regard it as their right to watch television every night, and see the quarrels as their mother's fault. Mrs Thomas can provide all sorts of rationalisations for her behaviour, however, and is very convincing, so that an impartial observer would probably decide in favour of whichever side happened to have spoken last.

We can only see what is really happening, see beneath the surface, if we do not allow ourselves to be blinded by the facts. These days facts are commonly overrated, but 'facto-philia' is so widespread only because it offers magnificent excuses. It allows people to forget that the interpretation of the facts, how the facts are used or misused, is much more important than the facts themselves.

The Thomas family are misusing the fact of the inter-fering mother in order to become indignant, and depict her as stupid, unfair, bad and guilty. If they would only look beneath the surface, they would be able to recognise how their deeply discouraged mother is waging a desperate battle against her isolation in the family. How simple it would be to give her what she needs: appreciation.

And Mrs Thomas misuses what she sees as the fact of the television. Because she believes so little in herself she thinks it necessary — unconsciously, of course — to disparage the behaviour and actions of the others by criticising the television.

Both sides have decided in favour of negative feelings, negative motives, conflict and reaction. The recognition of these forces below the surface and an appreciation of the mother's low opinion of herself could lead to an immediate improvement in the situation. The initiation of a family council (see Chapter 22) might also help.

Mr and Mrs Parker are planning to go out. Mr Parker reminds his wife that she must be punctual this time so that their friends are not kept waiting again. Ten minutes before they are due to leave it is clear to Mr Parker that his wife will not be ready on time. He becomes nervous, feels unfairly treated, and gets annoyed. Angry words are exchanged, and they find themselves in a battle over things that have nothing to do with going out, her un-punctuality or his impatience.

31

It would appear that Mrs Parker's unpunctuality is to blame for the argument, but beneath the surface we are aware that both of them are experienced warriors, well co-ordinated with each other. It is unimportant who it was that started the argument. It has nothing to do either with the wife's unpunctuality or the husband's impatience; both are merely weapons in a mutual power struggle. In this struggle Goal Three is being pursued on both sides. Each puts down the other in order to gain superiority — this is the real force below the surface.

Instead of expecting his wife not to be punctual and provoking her with his apparent concern, Mr Parker might consider whether he could give her a hand, do something for her, help her. Then she would have some encouragement to be punctual. If for some reason she really does find it difficult to be punctual, they could discuss in a supportive way what could be done in order not to keep their friends waiting. Mr Parker might go ahead, for example, leaving his wife to follow later.

If we do not take the facts too seriously, but see instead what is going on beneath the surface, we can understand ourselves better, and be better understood. We can create a situation where we are working with each other rather than against. If Mrs Parker tried to imagine how things were for her husband rather than for herself, and attempted to see the situation as a whole rather than as her problem, then punctuality would probably cease to be an issue between them.

6

LEAVE THE PAST BEHIND

*'When criticism and harsh words arise within a community,
there is no remedy except to put the past behind'*[12]

Mrs Rose and her sister are enemies. Many years ago
there was a bitter argument in which Mrs Rose judged
her sister to have behaved extremely unpleasantly. It
reached the point at which the sister's name could not be
mentioned in Mrs Rose's presence. Mr Rose went along
with his wife's game, and both did everything they could
to prevent contact between their children and the sister.
In the long run, of course, this was impossible. When the
children grew up they found the 'hate for all time'
absurd. Today they have normal family ties with their
aunt, which their mother resents.

Mrs Rose has no idea why she cannot forget the past. She
cannot admit, even to herself, that she feels herself to be
morally superior to her sister, or that she wants to remain
'the better sister' for ever. Whether the sister really behaved
so badly at the time, or whether there was a series of mistakes and misunderstandings, does not matter any more.
Mrs Rose is convinced that her sister is to blame.

A year ago Mr Sharp ran over and killed a child. The
police investigation and subsequent legal proceedings

have proved beyond a shadow of doubt that he was completely innocent. Nevertheless he cannot get over the fact that he has killed a child. Mr Sharp still cannot bring himself to sit behind the wheel of a car again, even though this makes his business life extremely difficult.

It is very easy to understand when someone goes to pieces after the shock of such an accident, and easy to see why he would not want to drive a car again immediately afterwards, but when over a year later he is still perpetuating the effect of a shock, he must have some investment in doing so. Does he not believe himself capable of success in his business, and thus have a welcome excuse to fail? Does he enjoy the attention evoked by his behaviour from his family and business colleagues? Or does he achieve a feeling of superiority: 'See what a good person I am, compared with others who would behave less sensitively'? Or is he looking for revenge on someone — his wife perhaps, because she encourages him to be successful in his business? If he could be helped to recognise which goal he was pursuing with his unusual behaviour, he could probably change his decision.

Mr and Mrs Edwards often quarrel with each other. After each quarrel Mr Edwards writes down an exact account of everything his wife has said. After all, you never know when it might be useful.

Mr Edwards is showing that he has no real faith either in himself, or in his wife, or in the stability of the marriage. By writing everything down he wants to insure himself against future uncertainty, and does not understand the extreme insecurity displayed by his behaviour. He is standing in the way of any improvement in the marriage, because he is expecting the relationship to fail.

Adenauer once said: 'To fall is neither dangerous nor shameful, but to remain lying down is both.' So many people insist on staying down, clinging to the past. How many bad thoughts and feelings arise because a person keeps remembering what someone else has said or done? Causes may be interesting, but they are of little practical help in choosing how to face the future. All that can help is the decision not to let yourself be too strongly influenced by the past, to do your best in the present, and to recognise your goals for the future, changing things for the better all the time.

And what do we do with the guilt? Notwithstanding popular opinion, guilt does not help us towards more positive action. Guilt perpetuates selfish and inappropriate behaviour.[13]

Mrs Innes, who is fifty, lost her husband three years ago. She lives alone, and both her children are married and live far away. She feels more and more isolated, and has the feeling that the friends and acquaintances she used to have in common with her husband are gradually deserting her. At the same time she is aware of the prejudices that people have against a single, no longer very young, woman. As a result she is full of bitterness, and complains to the few people who still listen to her about the wickedness and unfairness of the others, about life, fate, and her own hard luck.

Mrs Innes does not understand that she herself is to blame for her own loneliness. No one listens gladly to someone else's eternal complaints. Losing one's partner is perhaps the worst thing that can happen to a person, but should you really let it get in the way of living in the present?

Mrs Innes can change neither the past nor other people, but she can change herself. She can make an effort to change her attitudes to life and to other people, and especially to herself. Firstly, she should learn to value herself as a person in her own right, rather than in her rôle as a wife only. She might also consider the fact that she is still relatively young — why should she not remain open to the possibility of finding another husband? After all, she still has nearly half her life ahead of her. She can set her sights positively.

Mr Graham has just had a big celebration for his seventieth birthday. He still has a whole crowd of friends, with whom he is popular. He is a good entertainer, fond of telling jokes, but he does talk a lot about the past, about the War, about the important position he had: 'Oh yes, it was certainly different then . . .'; 'In those days we would have . . .'; 'Young people today . . .'. All these are standard phrases in his repertoire. No wonder he doesn't get on well with his own children, nor any young people for that matter. He is no longer taken seriously by them, and so becomes increasingly bitter and negative.

Sometimes it isn't easy for older people to understand that there is no intrinsic merit in white hair. Even the number of years behind you and your past achievements do not entitle you to claim special rights or privileges, special consideration or recognition, inappropriate honours or authority. If you make such demands, you will slowly but surely isolate yourself and make yourself appear ridiculous.

Older people too must consciously live in the present. The greater their knowledge, the greater is their responsibility to pass this knowledge on. If older people believe in themselves, they can contribute to society until the end of their lives, and contributing to other people is what makes us really happy. The older you are, the more you realise that it is better to give than to receive — working to make other people happy is the greatest virtue.

7

NEITHER QUARREL
NOR GIVE IN
BUT UNDERSTAND
AND WANT TO HELP

'Of all men the most negligent is he that disputeth idly and seeketh to advance himself over his brother'[14]

Today's world is full of conflict, struggle and war. Wherever we look, whether on the small scale of families and classrooms, offices and workshops, clubs and associations, or on the large scale of communities, nations, races and religions, we see not only open 'hot' war everywhere, but an enormous amount of conflict beneath the surface, the 'cold' war of verbal duels and disputes, fine barbs aimed to hurt.

In all of this it is obvious that nothing can be achieved through conflict and quarrel. Conflict begets further conflict; war begets further war.

There are people, particularly the good and lovable wives and mothers, who give in 'for the sake of peace' in order to avoid quarrels. Any other course of action is unimaginable: either quarrel or give in. Giving in, however, is just as bad as quarrelling. In quarrelling I insult the worth of the other person; in giving in I insult my own worth. If I believe in the social equality of all people, then I have a duty to consider my own worth just as much as that of others. Mutual respect, without which a balanced and harmonious relationship is unthinkable, shows us a third course of action: to understand and be willing to help.

If I understand the goals other people are pursuing with their negative and provocative behaviour, why they choose to disturb the relationship between us, then that can help me to react less to their behaviour. As a result it becomes less important to me who they decide to make into a scapegoat and who they want to blame — instead I can consider whether and how I can help them. After all, it is the person who is behaving in a disturbing way that needs the help, not the one observing that behaviour.

Mr and Mrs Grindley play the same game every night, and both know the rules well. She claims that she cannot go to sleep without having read for a while, and he complains that he cannot go to sleep with the light on. This happens every night, and every night they end up quarrelling. When they are tired of battling they both go to sleep thinking evil thoughts, ready to continue the war at the earliest opportunity the next morning.

If they were to ask their friends for advice, the friends would surely offer some useful suggestions: they could buy a bedside table lamp which would not disturb Mr Grindley; or he could wait until she had finished reading before going to bed; or they could have separate bedrooms. Each of these well-meaning suggestions overlooks the real problem. Both of them are convinced they are right, because being right makes each of them feel — unconsciously — that they are superior.

Every quarrel begins when one person who wants to be right finds a second person who also wants to be right. Important though rightness and the administration of justice may be for social relations in larger groups, they are usually harmful in small groups such as families. If someone in a family conflict is right, then he or she should be satisfied with that knowledge and consider how the other person can be helped. If, however, it is more a question of proving rightness rather than simply being right, then they put themselves in the wrong, however right they may be! Anybody who is interested in proving his or her rightness is interested more in self than in the other person. Right should serve the person, not the person the right.

Two quarrelling people create a vicious circle as long as each wants to prevail upon the other to give in. Only one thing can help: to take the first step yourself.

If Mr and Mrs Grindley had a positive attitude to each other, each of them would think about the other and not about themselves all the time. Mr Grindley could be satisfied with the knowledge that he does not need to read in order to help himself go to sleep, and be glad that his wife has such simple method of overcoming her difficulty in falling asleep. If Mrs Grindley wanted to be the understanding one, she could take the first step. Instead of reading, she could lovingly and understandingly talk with her husband, convinced that such a conversation would help her fall asleep just as surely as reading. She could also consider why her husband is so sensitive to the light. Does he feel ordered about and manipulated by her?

Mr Smith is sitting at breakfast; his wife appears from the bathroom. She looks annoyed, so her husband asks her what's wrong — she seemed in a good mood before she went in.

'Nothing, there's nothing wrong. Why should there be?'

'I can see it in your face.'

'Oh, leave me alone.'

'Come on, you can tell me.'

'Okay, I will. I've told you time and time again that I

can't stand it when you squeeze the middle of the tooth-paste tube. Why can't you squeeze it from the bottom? Every morning I have to waste time getting it all back up to the top. You're just a slob.'

'Oh, come on. Don't be so particular. As if it was important how I squeeze the toothpaste tube! I've just about had enough of your nagging . . .'

He has worked himself into a state too, and now the quarrel really begins. They both know their lines perfectly. In the end he leaves half his breakfast and storms out of the house, while she falls into a chair, exhausted, and plots revenge.

There are, of course, any number of clever suggestions in this situation too: Mrs Smith could buy her own tube of toothpaste, for example. But again it is essential if they are to break this cycle of conflict to understand each other, to recognise each other's motives. Many people will sympathise with Mrs Smith's reaction to her husband's slovenliness, but nothing can be achieved by anger. All that can help her is the realisation that she has generated her anger in order to criticise her husband for his untidiness, and to achieve superiority for herself by basking in the splendour of her love for order. If she were to look at the mistreated toothpaste tube with this realisation when she goes into the bathroom the next morning, she could not become so angry again. Being angry with someone else is simply less easy when you have seen through yourself and your own motives.

Her husband, too, could contribute to the peace. Instead of letting her challenge him to a fight, he could inwardly grant her the right to her anger, and outwardly take her lovingly into his arms and say that in future he will try to be more considerate of her wishes. This has nothing to do with giving in; it has to do with love and understanding for one's partner.

40

George and Brian are spending the evening together. George says something which Brian realises immediately is stupid, because he happens to have a detailed knowledge of the subject. Brian points this out to his friend, but George reacts vehemently. 'You always have to know better!' he says. Now both of them feel on the defensive, needing to justify and defend themselves. When they part they are still angry and annoyed.

If George had really said something stupid, Brian could have continued to listen attentively in order to find out his reasons for making the statement, since Brian knows that George isn't prone to stupidity — why would they be friends otherwise? Perhaps he can learn something from George's remark, or from the way that George formed this particular idea. He might get to see some aspect of the issue that he hadn't thought about before.

What if George was just bluffing? Brian could still try to understand why his friend felt he needed to do this — to conceal his insecurity, perhaps, or that he fears being inferior and wants to appear superior. When he had understood this, Brian could have thought about ways he might encourage and help his friend.

Ray is twenty-seven. He has come to know a young divorcée; they share a lot of interests, and meet regularly at his flat at weekends and in the evening. At her wish they become engaged. Three weeks later, while they are on holiday together, she suddenly declares — without any warning — that she would like to have her own room. She has had her own room since the divorce and has got used to it — to have to share all the time would take away her privacy.

Ray went along with her wishes, as he usually did. She took a room for herself, and behaved in a rather reserved

41

way for the next few days. Even though he tried to be friendly, conversations seemed to end in bad feelings after a very short time. He continued to be polite and respectful, but although he was careful not to force himself on her at all, she was often childishly aggressive and sometimes quite offensive. She ignored the way he was feeling, and dismissed his attempts at conversation as ego stroking. They travelled back separately.

She had always said that she would be a bad housewife, and she had no interest in children. When problems in her previous marriage had arisen she had given in easily — the marriage had only lasted a few months. Ray, however, continued to see her, even though he sensed a coldness of heart and an inability to take the wishes of a partner into account.

Physical contact was only permitted when she wanted it. Ray attempted to compensate for his fiancée's insecurity and demands for assurance by always being available to her and by introducing her into his family. He was careful never to control or limit her. He did everything he could to demonstrate how much he loved her — he even made her his sole heir.

Ray was glad when she accepted all this, and continued to be careful not to exert any pressure on her at all. In the last ten weeks he has written her six letters, and has heard nothing in reply. He no longer knows what to do next.

Ray is allowing himself to be tyrannised by his fiancée — he is constantly giving in. But she can only play the tyrant if she can find someone willing to be tyrannised, prepared to play the rôle of slave. The 'slave' is just as much responsible for this state of affairs as the tyrant. He or she is permitting the tyrant to behave badly, and in the long run stands in the way of the tyrant's further development.

42

Why should a person change when the tactics they are using are proving successful? What can someone cast in the rôle of slave do? Fight? This is as poor a solution as giving up. Think about the following:

1) We must remain friendly (act), and not let our behaviour be dictated (react), or let ourselves be challenged to conflict and quarrels.
2) We can say: 'I don't agree with you, but perhaps you have a point. I will think about it.'
3) We then do what we consider to be right.
4) We must understand that a tyrant only feels the need to act like a tyrant because he or she feels insecure and is afraid of being inferior.
5) We must consider how we can help and encourage that person.

We cannot, however, make anybody change by forcing them into undignified submission — that will only encourage them to continue with their destructive behaviour. The only thing that will help is to behave in ways which will show that we believe in people. This is not always easy, however, and possible solutions are discussed in the next chapter.

Let us return to Ray and his problem. Does he really want to get married? And is his fiancée just too much of a problem? Perhaps both of them are fearful of marriage — she does not want to be in the inferior position of a wife, and he does not have the confidence to play the supposedly superior rôle of a husband. As things are going, each of them represents for the other a wonderful alibi for avoiding marriage, because each is convinced that it will be the other's fault if the marriage never happens.

This may sound fantastic, but not if we look beneath the surface. Ray's fiancée has probably been told as a child that she is 'only' a girl, and has learnt that being a girl has

43

disadvantages. The fear of continuing to play an inferior rôle has given her a fear of marriage. Young women with this fear may well choose a marriage partner for the wrong reasons. Either they fall in love with a married man, as happened several times for Ray's fiancée, or with a man who — though looking for a partner — is inwardly set on avoiding marriage. Seeking the perfect partner, who of course does not exist, leads to outward failure which is also an apparent inward success (see 'Masculine Protest', Chapter 23).

When women with this fear of marriage find a partner who from all appearances seems to be right for them, something is still missing — they do not form any feeling of attachment, which is the most important factor in any choice of partner. In Ray she has found a man who appears to be prepared to give in and be her slave, but her fear is so great that she draws back. If she had ever managed to get him to marry her she would always have had the perfect excuse to blame him if things went wrong. After all, it was him that wanted to get married; she always knew it wouldn't work.

If Ray had given in, it would have been easier to separate from his difficult partner and look for someone else. If he really wants to get married he will surely be able to find someone for whom he does not need to sacrifice so much or put himself in such an undignified position.

Of course it is right that he wants to help her, provided he really is looking for a marriage partner. Either he must continue to show love towards his fiancée without letting himself be manoeuvred into an undignified situation and with the understanding that she will seek professional help and advice, or he must give her up. He cannot change her.

A mother of twins recently told me this story:

She overheard one saying to the other, 'I'm the I and

you're the you.' Then the other said: 'No, I'm the I and you're the you.' In a louder voice, the first repeated: 'No, *I'm* the I and *you're* the you!'. So it continued, getting louder and more excited all the time.

Here are little children demonstrating the need to be right. In order not to perpetuate this way of relating it is very important for parents to learn to discuss things with each other (Chapter 9) and to come to an agreement despite differences of opinion (Chapter 10).

To end this chapter, here are some more thoughts:

Other people are fellow human beings, not competitors.

What matters is that we are friendly and firm at the same time: friendly to others and firm with ourselves, both in what we decide for ourselves and in what we want to achieve. We do not need to strive to be right.

Being wise means to understand and to help, not to give in.

Never tilt at windmills!

8

DISTINGUISH BETWEEN
THE DOER
AND THE DEED

'You must . . . be kind to all men; you must even treat
your enemies as your friends. You must consider your
evil-wishers as your well-wishers. Those who are not
agreeable toward you must be regarded as those who are
congenial and pleasant so that, perchance, this darkness
of disagreement and conflict may disappear from amongst
men and the light of the divine may shine forth'[15]

However badly a person may behave, he or she is still our fellow human being, our brother or sister, with a right to our respect. I can reject the behaviour, but not the person. Yet we often make this mistake. A child that I reprimand or scold for being naughty can feel rejected by me, which can have a very discouraging effect. Thus before I reject the child's conduct I must first reassure him or her that my love for them is just as strong as it was before their misbehaviour. If only we could put this rule of social conduct into practice, this rule which all religions teach — love thy neighbour as thyself. Loving our nearest and dearest is something we find easy to understand, but to love all our neighbours, which is necessary for social interaction at every level, is something we can only do when we see each person independently of his or her words and deeds.

Mrs Gibbs and her mother go to a Chinese restaurant. She orders the special chop suey; her mother has chicken and chips. Even before the waiter brings the meal, her mother says 'Oh dear, I think I've ordered the wrong thing. Yours looks much more interesting. I always do that.' And of course when the food comes she doesn't enjoy it. She would have much preferred what her daughter has ordered.

When she sees her daughter again two days later she brings the subject up again. She really regrets having paid out good money for that meal, she tells her daughter. Mrs Gibbs is annoyed by her mother's dissatisfaction. 'I can't bear it,' she says. 'You always criticise everything, and I don't get any pleasure from it at all.'

It is neither easy nor right to tolerate this sort of negative behaviour. On the other hand, if Mrs Gibbs could distinguish between the mother and her behaviour, she could reject her mother's conduct without rejecting her mother. Out of her love for her mother she can understand that her mother is unhappy and needs help. She can then consider how she can help her mother to be happier, and at the same time she will find her own anger decreasing.

She could think about how she could bring some joy into her mother's life. The next time they go out together she could suggest that they both order the same thing, or that they might share the two dishes. Her mother would probably still find fault with that, but if Mrs Gibbs does nothing and acquiesces with her mother's behaviour, then it is unlikely that things will ever change.

If we are open to doing something to help, many more possibilities present themselves than when we are merely reacting, acting to hurt. Perhaps the mother only wants to be comforted, so why not give her some comfort? Perhaps

47

she wants to be admired for being such a wonderful woman, despite all the things that seem to get in the way. Perhaps she is just comparing herself with her daughter, who seems to have had everything so much easier; she feels she has had the short end of the stick and feels — unconsciously of course — that she needs to punish her daughter. Whatever the reason, Mrs Gibbs can free herself to help her mother by separating the person from the behaviour.

Mr Jones and his wife are at a social gathering. At first he graciously draws her into the limelight, introducing her proudly, because she is very attractive. Soon, however, he starts to monopolise the conversation and ignore her, not letting her speak and interrupting her when she does. On the way home he asks her, offhandedly, if she thinks he made a good impression.

The same thing happens again and again — Mr Jones is very self-centred and in need of recognition, and Mrs Jones allows herself to be manipulated by him, gritting her teeth at the same time. If she were to differentiate between her husband and his bad behaviour, she would not become so discouraged, and would become more self-confident in social situations. She would come to understand his little-boy showing off, so obvious from his behaviour after the party. Instead of getting angry, she could inwardly smile at it, and help to inject some courage into him so that he would gradually come to rely on this sort of behaviour less and less.

Mr Underwood has a neighbour who is forever piling all sorts of things against the boundary fence between their houses. This frequenty results in rubbish coming through the fence onto his side. When he objects to this, his neighbour is uncivil, and tells Mr Underwood not to make such a fuss.

The neighbour is inconsiderate, and Mr Underwood's objections meet with no success. Mr Underwood is not only provoked by him, but talks disparagingly about him, and even starts to plan his revenge. He certainly considers himself to be right, and thinks about seeing his solicitor. Whatever Mr Underwood is thinking of doing in this direction, it is bound to cause trouble and ill feeling. If he takes revenge by throwing his rubbish into his neighbour's garden, the battle will only intensify. If he decides to prosecute, it will cost a great deal of time and money, quite apart from the fact that he would know that he had not really dealt with the situation. Verbally running his neighbour down won't help either — anyway, Mr Underwood is too intelligent and sensible to do that.

If he could separate the person from the deed, reject his neighbour's behaviour while respecting the neighbour himself as a fellow human being, he could try to speak to him (see Chapter 9). During the conversation he could emphasise his neighbour's positive qualities. When his neighbour feels how positive Mr Underwood's behaviour is towards him, this could in itself form the basis for causing him to show more consideration towards Mr Underwood.

9

TALK TO EACH OTHER

'When differences present themselves, take counsel together in secret, lest others magnify a speck into a mountain. Harbour not in your hearts any grievance, but rather explain its nature to each other with such frankness and understanding that it will disappear, leaving no remembrance'[16]

Talking to each other does not mean talking at each other, it does not mean talking over the top of each other's heads, and it does not mean talking at cross purposes. It is neither successive interruption, nor a speech, nor a sermon. True communication is the basis for negotiation and cooperation, for achieving complete unity, and is thus one of the highest and most spiritual forms of human interaction. Together with faith (Chapter 3) it is perhaps the most important method of improving a relationship, a method which can and should be used in most circumstances.

The themes of such communication are not the usual topics of conversation — politics, football, the opposite sex, cars, television, work, fashion and children — but 'you' and 'I' with the object of establishing the 'we'. The following guidelines work for all kinds of dialogue, but I will start by using the technique between a married couple, since it is in marriage that we can come closest to achieving the absolute 'we', total union with another person.

Some guidelines for negotiation

Mrs Pringle has problems, and is longing for her husband to come home so she can talk to him about them. When he finally arrives home and she begins to talk to him, he brushes her off with a bored gesture. 'Can't you keep your worries to yourself?' he says. 'You're always worried. Anyway, I have important things to do.' He leaves her standing there and goes into his workshop. She is humiliated and deeply disappointed.

The first guideline — which is being ignored here — is that each person should explicitly make it clear to the other that they always have the right to ask for help when they have a problem which they cannot solve alone.

Mr and Mrs Levy are devoted to each other, and are always interested in each other's problems, whatever they might be. Mr Levy has just got home from work, where he has been having problems, and he wants to tell his wife all about them. She, however, is busy with their new baby, their first child. She is conscious of his demand for her undivided attention, and because she is taken up with the baby, is annoyed by his demands. He too becomes frustrated when it is clear that she is not entirely at his disposal.

Neither of them have clarified for themselves that the 'always' of the first guideline does not mean that one person must always be at the other's disposal on demand. The 'always' only means that time should always be made, but at a time that is convenient for both the people involved. This is the second guideline.

One evening, Mrs Williams comes home from her evening class and finds her husband and the children in front of the television. The children should have been in bed hours ago, and Mrs Williams is angry about this. She waits until the children have gone to bed, then speaks sharply to her husband. 'You know when the children have to go to bed. We've talked about it often enough. Whenever I'm not there you forget that you're a parent and that parents have responsibilities. I can never rely on you! The children always get their own way when I'm not here.' Mr Williams starts to defend himself, and a full-scale quarrel is soon underway.

Dialogue should never be attempted while the emotional heat is still high, while one or both of the people are angry or excited. The person who feels attacked will inevitably dig his or her feet in and move onto the defensive. The desire to be in the right will almost always lead to conflict and verbal battle. The third guideline for dialogue, therefore, is: Do not try to force a conversation as long as negative feelings exist.

Mr Carter was frequently away from home on business trips, and this was a constant source of friction between him and his wife. He rarely took his wife with him, saying that he couldn't afford it. She was constantly telling him how inconsiderate this was, and he always defended himself vehemently. The quarrels never ceased, and there was always an icy atmosphere between the two of them.

Reprimanding a person is always wrong — it can regularly lead to quarrels, but never to dialogue. Mrs Carter could learn to be patient rather than pressing her case at every turn. Why can she not turn to her husband for advice and help? Is the problem that she does not know how to occupy her time when she is alone? In a true dialogue the partners consult with each other and can usually find a solution. Perhaps, with her husband's help, Mrs Carter can find an interesting hobby, or together they could find new friends that Mrs Carter could visit while her husband is away travelling, or Mrs Carter could find a job. There are so many possibilities. And maybe if, as a result of the dialogue, Mr Carter does not feel pressurised by his wife, he could arrange for her sake to make fewer trips, or to take her with him more often. The fourth extremely important guideline for dialogue is thus: Never come to your partner with his or her problem, only with your own problem.

When partners have learned to promote dialogue in this way, then one further guideline becomes important. Imagine that although all of the four guidelines we have already looked at are being observed, one of the partners gets angry during the conversation. This is when the fifth guideline should come into effect: Discontinue the dialogue at this point, so that the conversation can be broken off on friendly terms and returned to later. This is something which should be agreed from the outset. Everyone has the right to behave incorrectly sometimes — for example, to get angry. The other partner must accept this, and postpone solving the issue at hand for a while. The person who gets angry should not be made to feel that the other person is offended by their anger. Only in this way can the partners separate for the time being as friends.

Consultation
'The heaven of divine wisdom is illumined with the two luminaries of consultation and compassion.' [17]

Here is a brief list of thoughts and ideas which can help in dialogues between partners:

Listen.
Relate to your partner.
Do not put down your partner's point of view.

Accept your partner's viewpoint when you can see that it is correct and worthwhile, and do not hold doggedly to your own point of view at all costs.

Do not let yourself be annoyed by your partner's opinions.

See your own point of view as a contribution, but not as an unalterable fact.

Don't be afraid of your partner.

Express yourself freely.

Check your motives.

Speak briefly and to the point.

Do not say the first thing that comes into your head.

Do not muddle things.

Do not split hairs.

Do not set out to persuade.

Do not stubbornly keep to your own point of view.

Do not try to dominate your partner.

Try to come to an agreement.

Avoid self-centredness, prejudice and passion. Embrace love, sympathy and sincerity; respect, confidence and courage; openness, fairness and dignity; moderation, humility and civility; calm, restraint and patience; forbearance, responsibility and kindness.

None of these guidelines should be used purely as tricks or slick techniques. They can only function when the intention is honest and the motive pure and sincere.

10

AGREE DESPITE
YOUR DIFFERENCES

'Do not allow difference of opinion or diversity
of thought to separate you from your fellow-men,
or to be the cause of dispute, hatred
and strife in your hearts'[18]

Every human being is entitled to his or her own opinion. As no two people are exactly the same, neither do two people ever think exactly alike. Mothers often make the mistake of thinking that their little daughters must think and feel just like themselves, but from the very beginning every small child is an individual personality who can feel violated by such an attitude on the mother's part. Every human being is relatively free in the formation of personal attitudes, and even identical twins are no exception. Like any other individuals, each can have very different opinions.

Political and religious groups and organisations often require their members to adopt certain sets of beliefs or opinions, but in doing so they only betray their inner weakness and insecurity. This is true of any association which demands uniformity of opinion among its members, and can be equally damaging in such partnerships as marriages and families. Uniformity of opinion hinders development and progress. For this reason, two people who live together should be glad that they have differing opinions, since 'the shining spark of truth cometh forth only after the clash of differing opinions.'[19]

The 'clash' should not, however, be understood negatively as a clash of weapons and opponents, but as a wonderful opportunity to be able to learn from one another. Nobody knows everything, and nobody is superior to another person in every way. If we choose to we can learn something from every encounter, whether the other person is a child or an elderly person, a scholar or someone who is uneducated, an intellectual or a peasant. Every shade of opinion, regardless of whom it comes from, should be viewed as a positive contribution.

This is what we understand by agreement: affirmation of the differentness of the other person through respect, humility, patience, understanding and love. To be able to express our opinion is not only our right — it is our responsibility. No one is too noble or too lowly to believe that their opinion is not important.

Let us allow Tamsin to tell her own story:

'My mother taught me what I know about sewing and knitting. Until our tastes began to diverge, she made almost all of my clothes. After that I made everything myself, and made what I wanted. One of the things I made was a really successful crocheted jacket. Everyone who saw it liked it — except my mother. She made it quite clear how hideous she thought it was.

However, one of her friends must have seen me wearing that jacket, because she told my mother how much she liked it and asked if she could have a closer look at it. The friend liked it very much, and wanted to make a similar jacket for herself. My mother asked me if I would show the jacket to her friend, and when I brought it out, she sat there with unmistakable pride in the fact that her daughter had made it'.

Tamsin's mother has no respect for her grown-up daughter, and it took a third person's opinion to persuade the mother to agree with her daughter despite their differing tastes. Tamsin has behaved correctly. She has not made her mother's problem — the fact that she did not like the jacket — her own. She granted her mother the right to decide what she likes and dislikes, but did not let herself be influenced. She did what was right for herself, and enjoyed making and wearing the jacket.

Two friends live together, and because they go to work at different times they have divided the household chores between them in the way that fits in best with their timetables. One of them gets home earlier, and so does most of the cleaning. The other does the shopping on the way home. Every morning he asks his friend to leave the big window open while he cleans, so the room will be well ventilated, but every day the window remains closed, and every day the friend has another reason for having forgotten.

Our daily lives often consist of such minor battles, and for many of us they can make living together very difficult. We frequently say things like: 'If only other people would do things differently, everything would be so much easier and more pleasant.' We know exactly what they would have to do to make things better, but we forget all the things that we could do ourselves. If the friend who does the cleaning thinks it is better to keep the window closed, this is his right, and I can only ask to have the window opened for a while. If I do this in a polite and friendly way, he is unlikely to have any objection, but if I keep telling him every morning what to do, is it any wonder that the window remains firmly shut?

In order to ask in a polite and friendly way, we need to have a positive attitude. I'm very glad not to be living alone,

I might think, and although I have a friend who for some strange reason likes to keep the window shut while cleaning, there are a lot of things I like about him.

Margaret has problems in finding a partner who lives up to her expectations and who suits her parents. He would also have to accept her father, a man who is fiercely independent and sometimes difficult to get on with. On the one hand she feels she would be prepared to deny her father for the sake of her partner, but she also wants to be loyal to her family — she always feels confused about how she can deal with the situation. She is convinced that this state of affairs could be dealt with if only she could find a partner who fitted in with her family.

Margaret has insufficient respect both for her father and for herself. She is struggling with herself. She probably doesn't want to get married at all, but unconsciously needs to find a partner just so that she can find fault with him. She will always find something which will not suit either herself or her family. She is approaching the choice of a partner with colossal misgivings.

If she really wanted to find a partner, there must be thousands of people who would be suited to her. It isn't a question of waiting for the one person who is ideally suited to be her other half. Everybody can adapt to another person to a far greater extent than most of us think is possible, and to adapt means to agree despite differing opinions.

Margaret is a very attractive woman who loves meeting people, and would have no problem in finding a partner. She can easily tell whether someone has the basic qualifications, or whether the differences in education, upbringing, interests and ambitions are too great. If she and her potential partner like and respect each other, why should her partner not be able to develop a liking and respect for her father too? And if both Margaret and her partner trust and believe in each other, surely it would be possible to win her father over by trying to understand the reasons for his attitude towards himself, other people, and the world in general.

It is Saturday afternoon. Marion has made herself comfortable in the flat which she shares with her mother, and is reading a book. Her mother comes in. 'You're not reading a silly book again, are you?' she says. 'How boring! Why don't you come out and drive into town with me.' This annoys Marion, and she replies touchily that she isn't bored, and anyway, the book is very interesting. 'Come on,' says her mother. 'You can always read books. Come with me.' 'No,' says Marion. 'I'm not going to be ordered around. Why don't you read something for a change? You never do anything useful with your time.'

Marion and her mother obviously have very different attitudes towards leisure time. Marion is understandably reluctant to let herself be ordered about, but she is not aware of the ways in which she reacts to her mother, and thereby makes herself totally dependent on her. Each of them wants to feel, and prove, that they are superior to the other, but neither of them will be happy doing things this way. How different things could be if they were to try and understand each other's point of view, and agree with each other despite the differences.

The mother could ask if Marion would like to go to town when she has finished reading; she could equally see what it feels like to go into town on her own occasionally. Marion could finish reading the chapter, then go with her mother. Or she could tell her mother in a friendly way that she wanted to read her book just now, but would be very happy to go out with her later, or the next day.

A prerequisite for agreement is mutual respect, and this is the subject of the next chapter.

11

RESPECT EACH OTHER

'Regard man as a mine rich in gems
of inestimable value'[20]

Mutual respect is one of the most important rules for a good relationship. Without this respect there can be no real equality between individuals or within groups of people. Without a deep understanding of equality and mutual respect, there cannot be peace.

Unfortunately, we have no tradition either of respect or equality. Until now, groups and communities have always had somebody who decided for the others, and who always had the last word. In a family, for example, it was usually the father, the patriarch, who controlled his wife, his children, and anybody else living with the family.

But this will no longer work, because more and more people are recognising that the principles of equality are vitally important, even within the family. Often, however, this realisation works better in theory than in practice, and we need to learn the techniques which can help us to increase equality between people in our daily lives. In particular, close relatives frequently have very little respect for each other — they know each other's faults too well and are often very failure-oriented. But we can learn the methods which can help us to avoid dissatisfaction, disharmony, quarrels and conflict, and mutual respect is perhaps the most important of these methods.

Seventeen-year-old Irene loves listening to music at all hours of the day and night. Her mother finds this very irritating, especially when she is busy or in a hurry — and Irene knows this very well.

This morning everything is running late. Irene's mother is in a hurry to get to work; Irene is late too, and tells her mother to hurry, but before she starts to get ready herself, Irene puts on a record. Her mother says nothing. When she puts the same record on for a second time, her mother asks her to turn it down. When it goes on for the third time, her mother cannot stand it any longer. 'You know it really upsets me to have loud music in the morning,' she says, 'and the same record three times is just too much!' 'Oh, Mum,' says Irene, 'I'm trying to learn the words!' 'Enough is enough,' says her mother, but Irene puts the record on again as soon as it has finished. Infuriated, her mother storms into Irene's room, picks up the record player and throws it on the bed, scratching the record badly. There is total silence. For the next couple of days they do not speak to each other.

When they do get round to talking about it, Irene claims that the first she knew about her mother's displeasure was when she came in and smashed the record player, and anyway, she had only played the record twice.

Mother and daughter are battle-hardened opponents, and the music is the strategic weapon. Neither of them has the slightest respect for the other, otherwise Irene could show some consideration for her mother and ask if it was all right to play the record, or wait until her mother had gone out of the house. Surely she could find times when her mother wasn't so busy and wouldn't be so irritated by the music.

If her mother had more respect for her, she could change her attitude towards the music her daughter likes, maybe listen to it with her and talk about it afterwards. She could think of her grown-up daughter as a friend, and learn something about the music which is obviously so important to her. Then perhaps Irene might become interested in listening to other music as well, music they might both like.

Her mother would never speak to her friends the way that she speaks to Irene. It is true that Irene provokes her mother, but why? Because she does not feel understood, particularly by her mother, and wants some attention. Her mother responds emotionally from her feelings of helplessness and powerlessness, and this gives Irene the sense of being right, which leads to a feeling of triumph over her mother. Her mother falls right into the trap. Each of them brings out the worst in the other, rather than helping to illuminate the 'gems of inestimable value' which each of them undoubtedly possesses.

Ignore backbiting
'That seeker should . . . regard backbiting as grievous error, and keep himself aloof from its dominion, inasmuch as backbiting quencheth the light of the heart, and extinguisheth the life of the soul.'[21]

Backbiting is another result of a lack of mutual respect.

The Zacharias's phone is in the hall, and because Mrs Zacharias speaks very loudly, her husband in the living room next to the hall can hear every word. As he listens, he can hear her complaining bitterly about one of their mutual friends. She has already annoyed him by going on earlier about this friend, who Mr Zacharias is quite fond of, and now he finds himself getting angry all over again. He finds his wife's tone of voice very overbearing, and doesn't like her making fun of their friend.

What could Mr Zacharias do to help his wife have more respect for her fellow human beings? He certainly cannot help if he tries to 'train' her, because nobody will listen if they sense that they are being coaxed. The most important thing he can do in the future is to refuse, in a firm but friendly way, to listen to any sort of gossip. He could say: 'I'm sorry, darling, but please don't think badly of me if I'm not prepared to listen while you backbite about other people.'

Respect yourself

An important part of mutual respect is the ability to respect yourself. 'The purpose of the one true God . . . in revealing Himself unto men is to lay bare those gems that lie hidden within the mine of their true and inmost selves.'[22]

It is naturally easier for the person who believes in God as creator to believe in him or herself too, for God can only be regarded as the embodiment of perfection, and will therefore not create anything which is less than perfect. As a creature of God I can be nothing less than perfect. The difficulty of this self-knowledge is associated with thinking in terms of levels of orders, and the knowledge that on my own level I am perfect, and that a sign of human perfection is that I can develop myself in almost unlimited ways. Compared with the lower orders (minerals, plants and animals) a human being is perfect; while compared to the upper orders (the spirits) we are still imperfect, and in comparison with God, who exists above the orders, we are absolutely imperfect.

But even the person who does not believe in God can see basic human equality as a basis for realising the worth of him or herself. Why should they alone be worth less than other people? This consideration should not, however, lead us to make personal comparisons of ourselves with other people, as we will see in the next chapter. Thought alone cannot bring about either self-respect nor the encouragement needed to gain it — this requires action and appropriate changes in behaviour.

When Christine got home from her seaside holiday she had a very sunburnt nose. She had bought some suntan lotion, but she hadn't realised she was so sensitive, and hadn't bought the right sort. When they met again, her best friend mentioned Christine's red and swollen nose, saying in a friendly way that she looked quite disfigured. Her friend also said that she would never have bought the lotion that Christine had used — she would have bought only the best.

Christine, who is never very happy about her appearance, was quite angry about what her friend said, and she asked her friend to stop looking at her and criticising her. 'I'm only interested in you,' said her friend. 'After all, we are good friends, aren't we?'

Christine wanted to be right, and felt angry about her friend's criticism. But we know that anger will never help things along. If Christine wants to increase her self-respect so that she can handle these 'criticisms' better, she could learn to admit her mistake — which was, after all, only due to inexperience — and ease the atmosphere with a humorous remark. It would also help her to recognise the purpose of her anger — to avoid feeling inferior to her friend. Her friend also wants to appear superior, but Christine could recognise this, too. Though they have different ways of showing it, both of them are pursuing the same goal, and this can never lead to anything except conflict.

Another thing that Christine could do is to look for the 'hidden gems', both in herself and in her friend. Instead of meeting criticism with further criticism, she can in future look for and appreciate the positive aspects of people.

12

DO NOT COMPARE YOURSELF

'The diversity in the human family, should be the cause of love and harmony, as it is in music where many different notes blend together in the making of a perfect chord.'[23]

It is easy to misuse the differences between human beings, their unique individuality, by comparing ourselves with others. This sort of comparison is always a sign that we do not believe enough in ourselves. Establishing that we are better than someone else or can do something better than they can is usually very useful when it comes to feeling superior. If, on the other hand, we can convince ourselves that other people are better than us, it can be a good excuse not to act or change.

We can, however, interpret the differences between people as a sign of healthy diversity, and recognise the unity that this brings. When I look at a beautifully laid out garden full of many varieties of flowers and plants, I can at the same time enjoy the individual plants and appreciate the overall effect — the unity in the diversity. Yet if I start to compare the individual plants with each other, and see how some are not as large or as colourful as others, I lose the overall picture.

It is the same with human beings. I can feel part of the whole of society, and at the same time rejoice in my own individuality and that of other people, without comparing myself with all the others. I can, of course, compare achievements, works and deeds — this can be a very useful stimulus — but if I transfer those comparisons to the people, it is bound to interfere with our relationships. If I am only using the comparison to bolster my own ego, then it can only get in the way of respect and understanding.

A student told me recently that he had trouble saying anything in a group. 'I often find myself thinking that I just can't say what I want to,' he said. 'I'm sure the others can say things much better than I can, and that they wouldn't understand me if I said anything. So I just keep quiet, even though I know people are getting the wrong impression about me and that I have some important things to say.'

Another student had similar problems: 'When I talk to the other students in my year I feel inadequate if I think they know more than I do. Quite soon we shall all have to write dissertations, and I really don't feel ready for that. I shall have to do it all on my own, and I don't feel I have the knowledge or experience to do it right. My friends all think I'm capable, intelligent and self-confident, but I don't.'

These are both ambitious young people who want to be better than others. Whenever they do something it must be as perfect as possible. Yet they both lack the confidence to do something which is important to them, so by comparing themselves with others, they find reasons which justify their underachievement and lack of participation.

Another student told me that her problem was how to approach other people. 'I don't think I'm as good as other people at showing my warmth and interest,' she said. 'I believe that honesty is very important, so I can't indulge in that sort of thing. I just withdraw. I'd rather watch them than get involved in the conversation myself.'

Making contact with other people probably creates more problems for us than any other aspect of our social life. This student compares herself with her friends, and has decided that she comes off badly. She is anxious when she is in their company, and worries about how they see her. The reason she gives — her belief in honesty — appears to be quite plausible, but it is not really the reason why she feels the way she does. If she stopped comparing herself with them, she could learn to accept that she was different. 'Okay,' she could say, 'I show less warmth and interest in people than some of my friends, but we're all different. I believe more in being honest.'

A group of young friends decided to read a book together and then discuss it, because they thought it was particularly interesting and important. Each of them read a section in turn, but when it came to one girl's turn she had only read a few sentences before she choked over the words, sighed, and said 'I can't read any more.'

She did not understand what had happened, but the two people who had read before her had read extremely well. She had always thought that she was better educated than either of them, so when her turn came she suddenly compared herself with them, and became anxious that she would not read as well as they had and that the others would notice.

The roots of this reaction lay in her childhood. She had grown up in perpetual competition with her older sister, which had led to continual comparison between them. This self-comparison had become second nature to her.

We can only learn to rid ourselves of the problems of

comparison by examining our motives very carefully, then forgetting our egos and becoming more objective, and finally, putting ourselves in neutral, which will be the subject of the Chapter 14.

Forget your ego

'When one is released from the prison of self, that is indeed freedom! For self is the greatest prison.'[24]

By the 'ego' we mean the 'little guy' in each of us who does not believe enough in him or herself, and is thus forever wrapped up in the constant fear of being inadequate. If we believe strongly in ourselves and what we have to offer as human beings, we shall be much more objective and not so occupied with our own egos. The more we believe in ourselves, the less seriously we take ourselves. The more we doubt ourselves the more we are wrapped up with our egos, and the more seriously we take ourselves, for the greater part of our attention is always taken up with whatever appears most important to us. This may seem paradoxical, and someone with very little self-confidence might be indignant if they were told that they were too concerned with their ego. He or she may think quite the opposite — that compared with other people, their ego is quite small.

We can forget our ego quite effectively if we can remember sometimes to tell it to take a back seat: 'I'm sorry, ego, but just at the moment I have better things to do than worry about you. Don't take offence if I leave you in the corner for a while until I have time for you again.'

Another thing we can do is to devote ourselves fully to the problem and its objective solution. More detailed guidance will be found in my book on self-education.[1]

68

Practice what you preach
'Let deeds, not words, be your adorning.'[25]

Both in his practice as a psychological counsellor and among his circle of acquaintances, Mr Norman talks a great deal about equality between people, and particularly stresses the importance of respecting the equality of young people. While many parents consult him about their relationships with their children, Mr Norman is not so successful in his own life — he finds it very difficult to cope with his eighteen-year-old son.

When his son comes home from work, he always goes straight to his room and turns the stereo on. Today Mr Norman is typing in his adjoining study. After a few minutes he cannot stand the loud music, so hammers on the wall. His son hears the knocking, and although he is angry too, he turns the music down a little, but he can never turn it down as low as his father wants it. This scenario has frequently led to heated arguments, and the son has told his father that the typing disturbs him just as much as his music disturbs his father. Both father and son use Mrs Norman as a go-between — 'You tell him!' they both say — and she lets both of them misuse her in order to perpetuate the bad relationship between father and son. They both feel they are in the right, and neither believes that there is a solution to the problem.

If, as usual, we start by assuming that practical measures have been considered, such as the use of rooms that are further apart, then we can look at the real problem. The father offers good advice to other people, but does not see how they apply in his own house. If he were to practise what he preaches, he could, by applying all the suggestions made so far in this book, see the situation more clearly and work towards an agreement, not generating unnecessary emotions, not harping on about his rights, respecting his son more, and talking instead of quarrelling.

Also, and very importantly for him, he would then be able to advise other people in similar situations with much more conviction, and therefore more success. His ego, which is not being acknowledged in his conflict with his son, stands in the way. Each quarrel with his son disheartens him because it confirms that he is not coping with the problem. It causes him anxiety because he feels defeated and not able to deal with the inevitable conflict.

Avoid double standards

'The wrong in the world continues to exist just because people talk only of their ideals, and do not strive to put them into practice. If actions took the place of words, the world's misery would very soon be changed into comfort.'[26]

We constantly apply double standards: we judge people according to their deeds, their actions and their behaviour, but we judge ourselves according to our feelings, thoughts and opinions. We employ different criteria for men and for women in order to 'prove' the inferiority of women and the superiority of men, a common belief even today. We call certain qualities typically 'masculine' and 'feminine', and exalt the 'masculine' ones. Or we establish double standards between adults and young people. To justify our own actions we distinguish between 'mature' and 'immature' behaviour, which in the final analysis is nothing more than an adult trick to feel superior and indulge in privilege.[8]

Then there are racial double standards, in which nothing is considered irrelevant when it comes to proving the superiority of our own race. Some Japanese, for example, consider their own race to be superior on the grounds that their sparce body hair proves them to be further evolved from the apes than any other race!

And then there is religious prejudice. In Christianity, our own religion, we are accustomed to an eternal divinity whose teachings never change, teachings which speak of the love of God and the importance of loving our neighbours. But many religions and sects are concerned very much with laws, commandments and prohibitions — the material, earthly, temporal aspect of religion which changes, or is transformed or abolished, with each new prophetic cycle. It is not difficult to see our own religion as superior in order to feel superior ourselves when we compare ourselves with the adherents of other religions.

We can acknowledge the senselessness of this way of thinking if we observe and practice the rules for harmonious relationships, and this new understanding of one another can be strengthened enormously through cooperation, which is the subject of the next chapter.

13

COOPERATE

'Today is the day of union . . . "Verily, God loveth those who are working in His path in groups, for they are a solid foundation." Consider ye that he says "in groups", united and bound together, supporting one another.'[27]

If we feel disappointed, or a failure, or any unhappiness in our relations with other people, then we can be fairly certain that the rules for social conduct have not been observed or have been infringed. The main cause for this is fear, which is a major obstacle in the way of any kind of cooperation.

Six rules for cooperation
1) A common goal must be agreed.
2) This goal should interest everyone concerned, and be worth their striving for.
3) The work should be clearly divided up, so that each person knows exactly what they have to do.
4) Even when everybody agrees that one person should be entrusted with leadership, responsibility must be borne in common by everybody.
5) As well as all formal agreements, there must be a readiness to give mutual help.
6) Each person must learn to involve him or herself 100%.

If someone is only giving 50%, they can very easily come to believe that they are giving 51% and receiving only 49%.

Although Mrs Dennis respects and loves her husband, she sometimes gets angry with him. He is very active, but their lively children quickly get on his nerves, so she frequently declines to join him in his activities, since either they do not fit into her schedule or the children have to be left with their grandmother.

Mrs Dennis ends up dealing with the practical details, and feels that it all lands on her shoulders. She feels very alone, and this is hardly to be wondered at, for she is not only responsible for the household — two children, two employees, her parents and her mother-in-law, but she also works part-time at the reception desk of her husband's medical practice.

Cooperation hardly enters the picture at all. Dr Dennis leaves almost everything to his wife, and considers himself to be responsible only for his actual medical work. He takes it completely for granted that his wife will involve herself in all his other projects.

What can she do?
First of all she must understand that her husband is playing the part of a slave-driver because he has a need to do it. This means that inside him lurks a little guy who is not very sure of himself, and is compelled to seek affirmation of his power outside of himself. This realisation makes it possible for Mrs Dennis to change her attitude, and see that her husband needs help. Until now she has only asked for help for herself. However, this help must not take away from her time and health, otherwise it would be denying her respect and value. It must consist chiefly in her explicit acknowledgement of her husband and what he is doing. She might for instance consider whether she should

continue to help in his medical practice. It is usually an advantage when husband and wife can work together, as long as neither of them abuses the situation. Where this happens, however, the husband should help the wife as much as she helps him, and not with any kind of condescension, but with an explicit recognition of the importance of her work. To bring her husband to this realisation may not be easy. It will require patience, and above all her own conviction of the value of her work as well as of herself. There is no more important task than that of bringing up the next generation.

Mrs Oliver frequently complains that she does all the housework. When her husband wants to clear the table after a meal, however, she always says: 'Let it be, I'd rather do it myself.' If he comes into the kitchen to help she always tells him he's in the way, and that he just creates a mess.

Mrs Oliver puts her husband down in order to feel superior. Here again the first thing to be done towards improving cooperation is to help her partner and strengthen his sense of his own value, explicitly acknowledging the value of his work and expressing appreciation of it.

The following examples show how far things can go when people do not cooperate.

Twenty-three-year-old Gillian never takes any initiative in her work. She leaves everything to others, and only does exactly what she is told to do. Her workmates become frustrated and annoyed, which leads to constant friction and bad feeling towards her. Occasionally she takes steps to become more involved and think for herself, but it never lasts for long. Her passive and defensive behaviour continually give rise to unpleasant situations, which make her unhappy and make life very unpleasant for her.

Mrs Pritchard sometimes likes to go swimming in the evenings. In the morning before she wants to go swimming, she asks her husband if she can have the car that evening. Without even thinking, he almost invariably says: 'No, I need the car. I have a meeting.' When she points out that he could go in a friend's car, he replies that he is constantly having to depend on other people. She is offended, and says: 'All right, you keep your car. I don't want it anyway. I like going on the bus.' This exchange leaves both of them bad-tempered and irritable.

When they both get home in the evening they do not mention it again. Each of them sticks inwardly to their own point of view, ready for the next round of the conflict. On the rare occasion when Mr Pritchard does allow his wife to use the car — which he never does without some complaining — he always moans the next morning about how he didn't get to bed until one o'clock because the others didn't want to go home. Since he never comes home earlier than this when he does have the car, Mrs Pritchard is even more annoyed.

There is no true partnership without cooperation. Both Mr and Mrs Pritchard have a deep fear of being at a disadvantage, of receiving less than they give. If just one of them were willing to put their interests completely in their partner's hands, their partner would slowly change, whether or not he or she wanted to. This must not happen, of course, at the other person's expense, because if that happened the partner would be tempted to play the tyrant.

In a marriage, cooperation is necessary in all areas, but it is often not recognised as such, for example in sexual intercourse.

Mr and Mrs Stevens are both thirty years old and have been married for six years. They understand each other

75

pretty well, though now and again there are marked differences of opinion. Both of them are easily offended, and even small disagreements tend to bother them. Things do not work at all well when it comes to sex. If Mrs Stevens shows any desire for her husband, he often withdraws quite brusquely. He turns over and leaves her tearful and despairing. She feels — quite naturally — that he is being unfair and inconsiderate.

It should not be difficult for Mr and Mrs Stevens to learn to cooperate; sexual issues are discussed specifically in Chapter 23.

Mrs Brown is a single parent, and has to take in work to make ends meet, so the children have to help with the household chores. Sixteen-year-old Peggy has been given the task of preparing the evening meal, but things start going wrong. She lets the milk boil over, then the vegetables boil dry, and finally she spills coffee powder all over the table. She rushes through to her mother and tells her that she's fed up with cooking and doesn't want to do it any more. In the end her mother loses patience and tells Peggy's older sister — who is none too pleased — to finish cooking the meal.

The goal of Peggy's behaviour is presumably to attract attention. Until now her mother and sister have taken all the responsibility for providing food, and Peggy has never learned to be responsible for other people in this way. Also Peggy does not yet believe in herself as far as cooking is concerned. Her insecurity and the fear of doing something wrong are obstacles to cooperation.

In cooperation, what matters is courage and self-confidence, and a feeling of concern for and trust in others.

14

LOOK FOR THE POSITIVE

'*To look always at the good and not at the bad. If a man has ten good qualities and one bad one, to look at the ten and forget the one; and if a man has ten bad qualities and one good one, to look at the one and forget the ten.*'[28]

What does 'positive' mean? Is it that which is right, and if so, who decides what is right? We all live with other people in some way — even the hermit, if only with a book written by someone else or with his memories of the past — and thus we have to have some philosophy of life. The clearer our philosophy of life, the surer we can be that our attitudes and actions will be right. Even when we cannot be sure of what is right, a clear philosophy of life at least helps us to recognise what is not right. At such times it is a great help to know what we should not do.

I believe there are three criteria which can help us decide what is right. Individual psychology puts two of them at our disposal, namely courage and concern for others. Both of these are important to us as individuals, and I would refer you, therefore, to my book on self-education.[1] Courage in this context is a belief in myself. Do I do things out of courage or out of fear? Courage is the more correct motive for action, and is thus one of the positive influences on my behaviour, since fear is a negative belief. Concern for others can also be defined as a belief in other people. Do I act out of my concern for other people or out of self-centredness?

Courage and social concern both improve the way I relate to others, and demonstrate the correct use of that strongest of human powers, faith. If, for example, I choose a partner out of courage and a genuine regard for others, that partnership will probably be successful. If I choose out of fear and self-centredness, my choice will probably end in failure.

Only believers make use of the third criterion, because it has its roots in religion. It is the fear of God. Unfortunately, it is often assumed that this means we should be afraid of God, but this 'fear' has as little to do with being afraid as having awe has to do with being awful. A few words from Zoroaster show this clearly: 'As the righteous man, having died, approaches his goal, in the third night after his death a maiden approaches him at dawn, pleasing, well-formed, strong and radiantly beautiful. Then he asks, "You, most beautiful lady that I have ever gazed upon, who are you?" And she answers, "I am your fear of God. I am your good thoughts, words and deeds . . ." '

Fear of God is the belief in that spiritual principle which we call God. It is the acknowledgement of and love for God which can lead believers to do what is right, namely to follow God's will. As Bahá'u'lláh says, '. . . Fear of God commands man to do what is correct . . .' And it is that which gives more courage and confidence to the believer than to anyone else. If he acts out of the fear of God, he acts in the certainty that he is correct.

When we can acknowledge these three criteria, or at least the first two, courage and social concern, then we can equate that which is correct with that which is positive. Since it is we who give meanings to things, we can decide what appears to us to be positive or negative. All we have to do is set our sights on the positive. Only with a positive outlook can we conquer the colossal failure mentality of our

78

civilisation, its pessimism, its negativity.

Seeing the positive is so important because we cannot build on the negative. Sometimes we have to create something positive in order to have a foundation to build on, but this is only possible if we have faith, if we believe in ourselves, other people, life and nature. Many people today find this belief difficult, often because they do not have a fundamental belief in the spiritual principle we commonly refer to as 'God'.

Associated with this negativity is another seemingly paradoxical phenomenon — it would appear that negativity spreads much more quickly than positivity. Let us take contagion as an example. Everyone knows that some diseases are contagious, but there is also a phenomenon known to relatively few people — the phenomenon of contagious health. It is relatively unknown because it progresses quite slowly and is thus not so obvious. It usually takes a lot longer to earn money than to spend or lose it. Bad news spreads further and more quickly than good news.

Why should this be? Because we are more attuned to the negative, to faults, and are not yet sufficiently accustomed to believing in the power of the good and the positive. When we hear people passing judgement on the times we live in, they speak of fear, war, materialism, selfishness and pessimism. If we were to set our sights more positively, we could equally well see the achievements of our time: the courage to consciously come to grips with problems, the striving for peace, the search for spiritual truth, the readiness to give help, the optimism.

A positive outlook is crucial for social relations today.

Mrs Wilson is often embarrassed to go with her husband to meet acquaintances who do not come up to his expectations. For this reason she never takes him to see her relatives. She finds that he is not really interested in other people. He constantly interrupts, puts them down, demolishes them with his logic, and almost never yields a point — a common failing she finds in academics. If the people they have gone to visit have any humour or spirit, or if he believes they are 'his wife's sort of people', he will sit there for hours on end, not saying a word unless he is directly spoken to. Even then he only mumbles.

His rules of conduct seem to be that either he likes someone, in which case he can be nice, or he doesn't, in which case he has no qualms in making it quite clear. Though his wife makes clear distinctions for herself between people who are genuine in their friendship and those who are merely polite, he accuses her of being nice to everyone. When they get home, she is angry with him, but he just tells her how hypocritical she is. His grumpiness annoys her, and other people have mentioned his ill humour to her.

To a certain extent Mrs Wilson has recognised how important it is to have a positive attitude towards other people, but she has obviously not managed to do this with her husband. Most of us are unwilling to admit to ourselves that we are most interested in the flaws of those nearest and dearest to us. Each flaw in a partner makes it possible for us to feel less defective, and thus superior in that particular aspect. And we do not readily relinquish this apparent superiority, since we believe too little in ourselves.

If Mrs Wilson were to see her husband in a positive light, she would be able to admire and appreciate his understanding and his logic, turning to him more often and asking his opinion, encouraging him to participate in the conversation. If she were then to apply correctly the suggestions made in earlier chapters, he would soon be less grumpy, and she would be less annoyed.

Annie had booked a holiday at the seaside. Just before

she went the weather was awful. 'What can you expect?' said her mother. 'It is nearly autumn.' Her mother's depressing tone made Annie angry, and she told her mother how tired she was of her negativity. Now Annie was sure it was going to rain all the time. Her mother had an uncanny knack of finding things to depress her, and now she had done it again. 'Well,' said her mother, 'you're even better than me at predicting bad weather!' Annie had to admit that her mother was right, but not without remarking that she found her mother's negativity really depressing.

Annie's mother does have a negative outlook, but Annie need not react with anger and frustration, criticising and reproaching her mother. She fears being inferior to her mother, and is conscious of the power struggle, for which she is just as responsible as her mother. Annie could learn to regard her mother more positively. And there is nothing negative about the autumn! Even if the weather was bad, she could find interesting things to do. We give meanings to things; they do not give meaning to us.

Geraldine's mother was angry. 'Where have you been? I bet you've been hanging round with the boys again! You're going to get yourself a bad reputation. I'm really ashamed. Nothing but boys on your brain. And when I have so much to do! I have to look after everything. You never help with the housework. What's going to become of you?' Seventeen-year-old Geraldine sulks and says: 'That's the way you brought me up.' This inflames her mother even further. 'I can't endure this! You'll have me in the madhouse before long.'

Geraldine's father now enters the fray, already angry. 'You shouldn't be doing everything for her,' he tells his wife. 'She won't be grateful. Don't be bullied into doing it for her . . .' Geraldine goes into her room. Later her

81

mother comes and fetches her back into the living room where, lo and behold, she is as nice as pie to her daughter.

The mother is thinking of herself, as is the meddling father. Geraldine's parents are not thinking of their daughter's real welfare. If they were, her mother would treat her daughter as a friend instead of criticising her; she would emphasise her positive qualities and treat her as an adult, which she practically is. Then Geraldine would react differently to her mother, and her mother would not find it necessary to make amends for her nagging. Real communication between Geraldine and her mother is only possible with a positive outlook, and it is only with this sort of dialogue that her mother's views about boys and relationships will be respected and taken to heart by Geraldine.

Connie came to see me with her problem:

'When anything bothers me,' she said, 'I really feel sorry for myself. I sit in my room and listen to music. I get so involved in the problem that I end up thinking that everything is bad, and that my life is terribly hard. The only way out is to force myself to go and visit a friend, or go out for a while.'

Life offers limitless potential for seeing things positively, provided we believe that we can develop a positive outlook. Things go as badly for people as they fear they will. Connie could learn how a positive outlook could change her feelings. Instead of passively giving in to her feelings and artificially intensifying them, she could concentrate on positive things and do something different. It's good that she lets her friends help her, but does she also help her friends?

William is just about to leave the railway station when he sees a frail old lady struggling with two suitcases. Since he is in no hurry, he goes up to her and asks if he can help. She shrinks back from him in fear and terror.

This happens all too often nowadays. There are many people who have had such bad experiences with other people that they are quite unable to imagine that a positive attitude to other people is conceivable.

15

PUT YOURSELF IN NEUTRAL

'Success or failure, gain or loss, must . . . depend upon man's own exertions.'[29]

Four rules

Putting yourself in neutral means freeing yourself of the notions of success and failure, being independent of other people's judgements and recognition. I do what I can. Since improvement is always possible, I know that what I do is never as much as it could be, yet I also know that it is always good enough. The important things are:

1) To set yourself a goal.
2) To regard that goal as providing you with a direction for your efforts.
3) To work hard to give of your best.
4) Not to misuse the achievement or non-achievement of the goal in order to influence your feelings about your own worth.

Worth does not depend upon success, as today's achievement-oriented society would have us believe.

Mr Urquhart was appointed coordinator of a committee which was organising a conference. For several nights before the conference he could not sleep, fearing that the whole thing might be a disaster. What would the others think of him then? He would be sure to be blamed.

Mr Urquhart's anxiety and sleepless nights give him a sort of insurance — they justify the possibility of failure. But the organisation of the conference will hardly be improved that way. If he could put himself in neutral, make himself independent of success or failure and the judgement of other people, he would not only be able to sleep better, but he would also increase the likelihood of success. He could stop struggling with himself and stop wasting energy, and would have more time to spend dealing with the organisation of the job assigned to him.

Expect the positive
'There are imperfections in every human being and you will always become unhappy if you look towards the people themselves . . . Do not look at the shortcomings of anybody; see with the sight of forgiveness.'[30]

Putting myself in neutral is completely compatible with expecting the positive — that is, success. To expect something means to believe that it will happen, and we saw in Chapter 3 that faith is the strongest power we have at our disposal. Through my expectation, through my belief in success, I contribute still more to that success. If in spite of this I do not succeed, however, then by putting myself in neutral I can avoid simultaneously inducing in myself feelings of disappointment.

After a ten-year marriage, Mrs Jones is in the middle of divorce proceedings. She fears that after the divorce, their two sons, aged five and seven, will be influenced against her by her husband. He has never helped much in their upbringing, and she is unsure about the future of their shared task of parenthood.

85

Mrs Jones expects the negative, for fear is a negative expectation, a faith in failure. As long as she is afraid, failure is more likely than success. Her goal is the successful joint upbringing of the children, but it would be dangerous to pursue that goal at any cost — the setting of a goal means only to have a direction for your efforts. Without constantly feeling the scourge of the need to succeed, the compulsion to achieve, and thus continually struggling with herself, she will be able to give her best in a way that is most likely to lead to success, to act more effectively.

Do not need to be certain

'One must never consider one's own feebleness . . . The thought of our own weakness could only bring despair.'[31]

Being certain is a pointless task. To be human means to be uncertain. Putting yourself in neutral means accepting the uncertainty of our existence without using it as an excuse for failure.

Mr Fisher is the owner of a small factory, but he finds it hard talking to potential customers. He is always afraid of stuttering, and that makes him fall over his words. He is afraid of stating his own conditions, of going along with everything his customers demand, and of ending up without an agreement — in short, failure. He is also afraid of confrontations with his colleagues, and starts to stutter whenever he needs to discuss their performance or their departments' results. Whenever he has to announce economy measures such as overtime cancellations or redundancies, he can hardly control himself.

Mr Fisher is in a very responsible position, and this puts strong pressure on him to succeed. Even so, he will inevitably be more successful if he stops needing to be certain of success, and puts himself in neutral.

Be able to say no

'Man should know his own self and recognise that which leadeth unto loftiness or to baseness, to shame or to honour, to affluence or to poverty.'[32]

Mrs Nuttall lives alone with her little son. Her brother wanted to take his wife on holiday without their children, and asked his sister if she could possibly take the children for two weeks. Even though she knew she could not cope with more children, she could not turn down her brother's request.

She had already promised her son that he could put up his model car racing track in her small living room, and thought this would keep him and his cousins occupied. She asked the father of one of her son's friends to come and help sort it all out. He of course brought his young son with him. Soon, word got round the neighbourhood that the Nuttall's house was an exciting place to be, and before long there was a crowd of enthusiastic children in the living room.

Mrs Nuttall was supposed to be studying for a training course, but the noise and quarrelling made it impossible to work. Two days later, and with three children still on her hands, she was still trembling.

It is good when we can do favours for other people, but when we know that we just can't manage it, it is better to muster up the courage to say no. If we always say yes, the people asking the favours will no longer regard it as a favour. Her son and her brother's children will suffer from Mrs Nuttall's nervousness, and that will create more problems. She will probably end up blaming the children as well as her brother, and in the end her brother and his wife will not thank her.

Emma has just met a man whom she doesn't find particu-

87

larly attractive. When he asks her out, she cannot bring herself to say no even though she has no interest in him at all, and knows perfectly well how angry she will be with herself afterwards. She nearly always accepts when she is asked out, because she believes she should respect the men who ask her, but the men who ask her usually want much more from Emma than she is interested in giving. Her agreement often puts her in situations which are difficult to get out of without hurting the other person, since her inability to say no often goes as far as ending up in bed with men she finds basically unattractive.

People who cannot say no are often people who feel so insecure that they are constantly relying on affirmation by others. They only see any value in themselves when this value is confirmed repeatedly by other people. For this reason it is vitally important for them to please others, because they believe it would be impossible to bear it if people had a low opinion of them. Since it is impossible to please everyone, however, they often exhibit nervous symptoms to excuse their indecision. Mrs Nuttall escapes in nervous trembling; Emma chooses periods of deep depression.

Be prepared for the worst

After working hard at it, Erica fulfilled her ambition to gain her light aircraft pilot's licence. She trained in a large group in which she was almost the only woman. When she had done only sixty dual control flights, her instructor got out and left her to undertake her first solo flight — the first from the group of thirty-five to be allowed to fly solo. The flight went brilliantly, and everyone — including Erica — was astonished by her performance. Many of the men had to wait a lot longer before being allowed to fly solo.

Without really being conscious of it, Erica had developed a method for giving herself confidence, and her instructor noticed. From the very beginning, she imagined what would be the worst thing that could happen, and she knew that if that happened, she could do the right thing — even in her sleep: turn off the petrol, open the throttle, open the cockpit roof, check the parachute, bail out . . . She had built up a certainty in herself that she would always do the right thing. 'Come what may, I know what to do!'

Martin is a university student who had enormous problems when speaking to a large group. Without a detailed manuscript he would lose his train of thought completely, and if he looked up at the people he was speaking to, he would find it impossible to go on.

Martin would be able to cope with a good deal of his insecurity by learning to put himself in neutral, and thinking to himself ahead of time: 'What is really the worst thing that could happen? What would I do then? What would be the best thing to do in that situation?' At worst, he would be laughed at or ridiculed, but he could tell himself that nobody is born a master of his craft, and that he wasn't alone with his problem. The world will not fall apart, and his value will not be diminished because of his lack of experience. If the others do laugh at him — which is very unlikely — then they are making a mistake, and he should not let it influence him. Perhaps his behaviour can thus help the others to be more understanding and less malicious and aggressive.

Be humble
'Humility exalteth man to the heaven of glory and power, whilst pride abaseth him to the depths of wretchedness and degradation.'[33]

Being humble does not mean humiliating oneself. If one

89

really believes in equality between people, it can never be right for someone to humilate himself, or let himself be humiliated by others. Everyone, by virtue of their very existence, is of enormously great value, and should never allow his or her dignity to be undervalued. Being humble means serving others, but not as a slave; rather as a free, self-determining person who consciously decides to serve because he or she has recognised that serving others is more necessary than ever before.

Ursula and Pat share a flat. One day when Ursula comes home, Pat is sitting in the living room with a visitor. 'Would you like some cake?' asks Pat. 'Yes, please,' says Ursula. 'It's in the kitchen,' says Pat. Ursula can see very well that there is enough cake for everybody on the living room table, but goes through to the kitchen anyway feeling insulted.

Ursula's feeling of humiliation is her problem — she has decided to feel humiliated. She could just as well have joined them at the table for a few minutes and eaten her piece of cake there. Or she could have said 'Thank you. I'll leave you to talk,' and left the room in a friendly way. Nobody can be humiliated if they choose not to be. It is the same thing all over again. Because we believe too little in ourselves, we react sensitively to every situation in which it appears that someone is casting doubts about our value.

Pride is another typical reaction with which we hope to salvage something of our sense of worth. Being proud is as incorrect as allowing ourselves to be humiliated. In the final analysis, pride is unintelligent, while self-humiliation represents a kind of self-surrender.

Never give up
'Each man has been placed in a post of honour, which he must not desert.'[34]

Whatever situation we find ourselves in, it almost never pays to give up or run away. The fable of the two frogs is a useful lesson:

Two frogs, one young and one old, go for a walk at dawn and reach the rim of a large milk churn. Without thinking, they jump straight into it. The churn is half full of milk, and they cannot get out again. The two of them kick frantically.

Finally the old frog says: 'It's pointless to keep on kicking. We'll never get up these smooth slippery walls.' He stops kicking and drowns.

The young frog, too, sees no possibility of escape, but he keeps on kicking. He does not give up.

After kicking for what seems like hours, he is suddenly aware of having found a firm footing. One jump, and he is free!

What had happened? During his hours of kicking the milk had turned to butter! The young frog could not have foreseen it, but he did not give up. He continued to kick.

We can never be sure what the future will bring, even when the present seems very bleak. It may bring something we could not possibly have foreseen. The main thing is to do what we can, even if we sometimes make mistakes.

16

TURN BIG MISTAKES
INTO LITTLE ONES

'The complete and entire elimination of the ego would imply perfection — which man can never completely attain.'[35]

The less someone believes in him or herself, the more they can fall into the error of wanting to be perfect, that is, wanting to make no mistakes. Perfectionism is exceedingly discouraging, because we can never completely avoid making mistakes. To be human is to make mistakes. But even when we make mistakes, our actual worth does not suffer. All that is affected is our feeling of self-worth, and how we feel about our self-worth is up to us, even if it is largely an unconscious decision.

In the present age of failure mentality, everyone is brought up to make as few mistakes as possible. But if we really want to learn to make fewer and fewer mistakes, there is only one way: to turn big mistakes into little ones. This is the policy of taking short steps. If we can count every small advance as a real achievement, this way of thinking about change can be very encouraging. It should not, of course, be done in order to feel superior to others, but in order to move further towards our goal. The more we can encourage ourselves in this way, the less we need to be anxious about our mistakes.

If Martin, the student in the last chapter, concentrated on the small advances he makes every time he speaks in front of a group of people instead of harping on his mistakes, he could gradually overcome his nervousness.

Whenever Liz makes a mistake or believes that she has done something wrong, she is so angry with herself that it can take several days to get over it, during which time she tends to overlook other, often much more important, things. Her anger causes her to make many more mistakes than she normally would, which in turn makes her even more angry. She cannot see how to escape this vicious circle.

When we are angry with ourselves, we are in effect fighting ourselves. The purpose of Liz's anger is as an excuse to overlook more important things. We do not know why she wants to do this — it might be that she wants to excuse her inadequacies (including the imaginary ones!), or that she wants someone to pay her attention, or that she wants to show her superiority by not doing what she should, or that she wants to punish someone. Whatever it may be, if she really wants to change things she only has to forget the mistakes she has made, knowing that in the future she can make smaller and smaller mistakes.

Have the courage to be imperfect
'Remember not your own limitations . . . Forget yourself.'[36]

Mr Allen worked in a large firm, where it was his job to see that all the information, advertising and prospectuses the company sent out were written in clear and concise language. He did this exceedingly well, since Mr Allen was a perfectionist, who would rather check something ten times than risk letting something go which may have had a mistake in it.

His boss was more than satisfied with the quality of Mr Allen's work, but was not at all happy with the amount of work he could get through. Mr Allen's desk was piled high with unfinished work. Every time his boss mentioned the growing mountain of work, Mr Allen worked longer into the evenings, and even took work home with him. Eventually he was working most weekends, and his boss suggested that he should have somebody to help him. Because he could not keep up with his work, Mr Allen was rapidly approaching a nervous breakdown.

He turned to an old friend for advice, and the friend made it clear to Mr Allen that everybody is allowed to make mistakes from time to time. Suddenly he understood that underlying his striving for perfection was a fear and a belief that he was inadequate. Mr Allen took this realisation to heart, and though at first it wasn't easy, he started to read each document only twice before approving it. His work was appreciated nonetheless, and as he became accustomed to the new way of working, he found that he could get through all his work with no problem.

Mr Allen had found the courage to be imperfect, to understand that the world would not collapse because of one mistake, to realise that his worth was not measured by whether or not he spotted every single error. To know that we can make mistakes is an enormous relief.

Forget the feeling of helplessness
'Do not look at your weakness.'[37]

Mrs Lindsay's greatest problem is her husband's depressions. When he is depressed she finds it just like talking to a brick wall, and though she would gladly help him if she knew how, she cannot think what to do. On days when he is depressed she feels as if too much is being demanded of her, and feels a great emotional burden. She tries to hide her husband's depression from her children and relatives, his colleagues, and even the daily help. Occasionally, when she can take the pressure no longer, she flies into a rage.

This shows all too clearly the effect that one person's depression can have on their family. The depressive's weapon is an extremely effective one, even if it is used quite unconsciously. Yet no one can blame him for his depressions.

The true nature of depression becomes clear when we see Mrs Lindsay's reaction to it — a fit of rage, a reaction against her feeling of helplessness. But how can she help? First of all she must resist all temptation to make her husband's problem her own — a person with severe depression is always a case for professional help. If she can do this, she can forget her helplessness and calmly accept that which, for the moment, cannot be changed. This will make it easier for her to remain calm and comforting, and not to abet her husband's unconscious feeling of not being understood.

17

DO NOT EXPECT A REWARD FOR GOOD DEEDS

'A man who does great good, and talks not of it, is on the way to perfection. The man who has accomplished a small good and magnifies it in his speech is worth very little . . . People make much profession of goodness, multiplying fine words because they wish to be thought greater and better than their fellows, seeking fame in the eyes of the world. Those who do most good use fewest words concerning their actions.'[38]

The whole family is seated at the table. Sixteen-year-old Celia and her mother are serving the food and helping the two younger brothers. Celia's father is carving the meat, and he pointedly gives the best slices to his wife and daughter, explaining as he does so how self-sacrificing he is. He grumbles about the children's table manners, then magnanimously offers round what is left of the salad before taking more himself. Then he calculates what a similar meal might have cost in a restaurant . . .

Celia, of course, sees straight through her father's behaviour, and certainly doesn't respond with the reward he is asking for — her appreciation. Her father rewards himself by demonstrating his generosity. If he had offered his family the best of the meal out of love, then perhaps he would be appreciated, but it would have been much better to have served it to them in such a way that the others had scarcely noticed him doing it. In that case the good he did would stay with him, meaning that he would become more positive, and would be in a better position to do more good. For a more detailed reasoning of this principle see my book on self-education.[1]

Admit your own mistakes
'God . . . wisheth not the humiliation of His servants.'[39]

Oliver, a young teacher, had a very lively class with which he could not always come to grips. Once he became so angry with them that out of revenge he gave his pupils a class assignment which was much too difficult. When it came to marking the work, he had to give them all much lower marks than usual. He thought about it for a long time, then decided to admit his mistake openly to the class, and not count the assignment towards the term's marks. When he faced his class the next day to admit his mistake frankly and openly, instead of feeling in any way humiliated, he could sense a wave of sympathy from the children. He realised that he had won their confidence by renouncing his personal pride.

If Oliver had not admitted his mistake, the children would have seen him as an adversary, and challenged his authority whenever possible. But what matters even more is that if Oliver had kept his mistake to himself, had retained his negative way of thinking, had not given up his need to be right, he would have become even more negative, and less and less in a position to do what is good — a person is what he keeps to himself.

Admitting your mistakes never means degrading yourself.

97

18

DO INSTEAD OF TRY

'Human frailties and peculiarities can be a great test.
But the only way, or perhaps I should say the first and
best way, to remedy such situations
is to oneself do what is right.'[40]

Many people spend a lot of time working out what they should do, but do not believe in themselves sufficiently to be able to complete whatever it is that needs doing. These are the sort of people who are always saying, 'Well, I'll try . . .' But if we attack a problem in this frame of mind, we do not stand much chance of succeeding, because we are only doing it half-heartedly. As we saw earlier, it is more correct simply to do what is required, without thinking about the possibility of failure. We have to be prepared to fail (see Chapter 15), but we should not count on it.

Mr King has five children between the ages of sixteen and twenty. He has come for advice because he feels responsible for a deteriorating relationship with his children. The educational psychologist describes to him how a family council might work, and outlines exactly how this very sucessful method can be used. Like most parents, Mr King is not completely convinced — he thinks the family council seems too formal. But he hesitates mostly because of the fact that a council would mean renunciating sole responsibility, and therefore sole power. At the end of the session with the psychologist, Mr King says: 'Okay, I'll try it.'

These words make it fairly clear to the psychologist that this attempt at a family council will not succeed, at least not to begin with. He will arrange another session with Mr King in a few weeks' time to see how things are going, and to give him further encouragement.

Fifteen-year-old Alan is *trying* to smooth out the conflict between his parents, but increasingly he ends up in the line of fire, particularly when his father starts insulting his mother. Eventually Alan's mother has had enough of the crude and vulgar language, and entreats Alan to steer his father out of the room. Alan has to resort to physical force, and this leads to more conflict. Usually Alan is the stronger of the two, but these sessions can go on for more than an hour at a time. Alan is frustrated by his mother's behaviour, though she defends herself energetically. Alan also feels very bad about his father, and goes to try and speak to him. His father doesn't want to talk, and Alan's pleas only result in conflict breaking out all over again. In the end he feels even worse about it all. He goes to his room and *tries* to do his homework, but he finds it hard to concentrate because the quarrel is still going on inside his head.

Right from the start Alan doesn't believe that he can do anything, and this leads to the familiar patterns of incorrect behaviour — the interference, the resorting to physical force, wanting to speak while the emotional temperature is still high, the guilt and the mutual accusations.

As long as we really want to accomplish something, it is best to strike the word 'try' from our vocabulary altogether.

19

WELCOME DIFFICULTIES

'Men who suffer not, attain no perfection. The plant most pruned by the gardeners is that one which, when the summer comes, will have the most beautiful blossoms and the most abundant fruit.'[41]

Mrs Vivyan has a problem. Her husband has a very demanding job, and he often has to work at the weekends. When this happens she usually helps him, since this is the only time they ever get together. The reason for this is that when her father-in-law died, her mother-in-law came to live with them, and now they have no life of their own at all. The little bit of free time they do have is always spent in the mother-in-law's company. Whenever they go out there are three of them. Not even the intimate hours when they work together are completely theirs, because his mother offers to help too. In some ways Mrs Vivyan appreciates her help, but it does mean that she can never have an intimate conversation with her husband like they used to have. Mr Vivyan is very glad to have all the help he can get, and does not seem to be so affected by the situation. Mrs Vivyan cannot think of a way to ask her mother-in-law to allow her and her husband more of a life of their own. She believes that it would be too difficult.

Whenever the possibility of parents or in-laws living with a family arises, I generally advise against it. Even with the best will in the world from everybody concerned, and even when the intentions are good, it does not usually work out for two, or even three, generations to live together under the same roof. In earlier times such arrangements were possible, and often worked well. Today, however, the attitudes, views and values of people and of society as a whole change so quickly that there is often an enormous gap between generations, and we simply do not have the means of bridging that gap. 'The rapidity with which man is progressing increases century by century.'[42]

Let us just look at one idea, that of partnership, in order to explore these changes. Older generations find it much more difficult than younger ones to understand partnership as a democratic relationship, involving mutual respect and equality. Even dialogue between equals is not learned overnight. Mrs Vivyan should first discuss her problem with her husband, because in a situation like this agreement between husband and wife is essential. Any discussion with the mother-in-law only has a chance of succeeding if she is convinced that her son and his wife are in agreement.

Mrs Vivyan's other lesson in this situation, however, is that if we are constantly aware that something is difficult, it can quickly drain our energy. If we have a task before us and we are always telling ourselves how difficult it is, then we are in danger of making a mountain out of a molehill. It is much better to recognise from the outset that life is difficult, then we no longer have to keep thinking about the problems in individual situations. If we really want to achieve anything important, it is best if we strike the word 'difficult' out of our vocabulary.

Up to now we have been looking at difficult situations which can be changed, but there are also difficulties which we cannot deal with right away, or perhaps ever. As well as

101

remembering to have the patience to bear what cannot be changed, there are also other ways of adjusting to seemingly impossible situations. Bahá'u'lláh assured us that afflictions, trials, sufferings and deprivations are 'blessings in disguise', through which our inner spiritual powers are stimulated, purified and ennobled, since they teach us to have more faith.[43] Shoghi Effendi says that 'Failures, tests and trials, if we use them correctly, can become the means of purifying our spirits, strengthening our characters, and enable us to rise to greater heights of service.'[44] 'The troubles of this world pass, and what we have left is what we have made of our souls.'[45] A quote from 'Abdu'l-Bahá illustrates this particularly well: 'We should try to make every stumbling block a stepping-stone to progress.'[46]

For a long time Mrs Morris has been suffering from a terrible fear that she might lose her husband. She can see that she is beginning to age, and the first wrinkles are appearing on her face. Until now she has had a good relationship with her husband. He puts a lot of stress on outward appearance, and she has always taken care of herself, but she has not been able to help noticing that recently her husband often ogles pretty young girls. She has spoken to her husband about her anxiety, but he just dismisses her fears with a joke.

Growing older is something which really cannot be changed. Why should we want to, when we can change our attitude and regard it positively? Just as I can decide to see each day as the most beautiful day in my life, so I can see positive things in being older.

Before Mrs Morris talked to her husband about her fears, she should have:
— Seen the benefits of growing older.
— Seen growing older as a blessing in disguise.
— Used this understanding for her mental development.

102

— Been able to welcome the situation.

If she had talked to her husband after she had done these things, her motive would have been courage rather than fear. She could then have forgotten her anxiety, and reflected on how she could best help her husband, since he is the one who is behaving wrongly and thus needs her help in being able to develop further. What matters, however, is not who is behaving wrongly, but how we can behave correctly.

Elizabeth occasionally invites her ageing mother, who lives in the flat underneath her, for coffee or for a meal, but she does get very annoyed when her mother talks continually about little things which are of no interest to anybody but herself, especially when she has heard the same things a hundred times before. Although Elizabeth knows that her mother has nobody else to talk to, it still makes her angry when she knows that her mother wants her to respond to everything she says. She thinks her mother ought to be aware that she isn't particularly interested, and that she doesn't have the time to keep saying the same things over and over again. So her usual answer is 'I don't know', since she knows that if she really says what she thinks, her mother will disagree.

This is another situation which probably cannot be changed. Elizabeth could move away, but she would find it difficult to feel good about it. A woman of her mother's age probably will not change now, though Elizabeth can work to develop a different attitude to the situation. If she could do this, she could make both her own and her mother's life happier, since nothing makes human beings more happy than the awareness that we have been able to do something for somebody else.

20

'MAY' INSTEAD OF 'MUST'

'Through the restoring waters of pure intention and unselfish effort, the earth of human potentialities will blossom with its own latent excellence and flower into praiseworthy qualities.'[47]

When the alarm clock rings early in the morning and Eileen has to go to work, she always feels miserable, and would much prefer to go on sleeping in order to avoid this feeling. She has a ploy which lets her do this — she always sets the alarm for a few minutes earlier than necessary, so she can spend this time in bed, but this doesn't help the feeling, because she still knows she has to get up very soon. The miserable feeling usually lasts until she has left the house.

This is a very common situation of the sort where people do not realise, or will not admit, how much they are personally responsible for the state of affairs. 'I'm a night person,' they say, 'not a morning person!' It is much more convenient to see ourselves as the victims of our own predispositions — of heredity or unfavourable circumstances — rather than admitting that we can change things ourselves. There is no such thing as a night person or a morning person, even though the belief is widespread and often taken as fact;

there are only people who see their work and life as a series of 'musts'. These decisions are often taken in childhood, and are frequently influenced by the behaviour of other members of our family.

If a child sees its father or mother enduring their work, treating getting up in the morning as a burden, and announcing — usually loudly — how terrible it is that they 'have to' get up, 'have to' go to work, and so on, the child will soon imitate this, and will probably find it very difficult to change this negative view of the world into a positive one. But we can all make 'mays' out of 'musts' if we are sufficiently aware of the need to do so. Getting up and going to work can then be seen as a challenge rather than as a burden, a blessing, something we can look forward to.

When Nick has things to do which he thinks might be difficult, he often feels tired and finds it hard to get up in the morning. He isn't aware that this never happens during the holidays — then he gets up early and happily, because he has arranged to do things he really enjoys. Nick puts the difference between winter, when he gets up later, and summer, when he gets up earlier, down to the weather — another intelligent excuse which most people will accept and not see for what it really is!

Rosemary has discovered the 'postponement technique' — when she has an important deadline to meet, she always postpones doing what needs to be done until the last minute, then has to do it under extreme pressure.

Postponing the unpleasant is a popular tactic. Besides working on this problem with our familiar immediate goals (Chapter 2), overcoming the need to postpone is often helped by developing a more positive attitude towards our obligations, so that we can feel good about what we need to do instead of struggling with ourselves and with the situation.

Every day, Roger finds that when his girlfriend talks to him he has a problem in concentrating. His mind is always somewhere else — at work or on his studies. He blames his lack of attention on exhaustion and overwork, because he does not want to admit to his lack of interest. If his girlfriend criticises his behaviour, he just switches off and won't even discuss the situation with her.

Roger and his girlfriend are both still very young, but they are already acting in a way very common in married couples, where being together with your partner is seen very much as a 'must', and not as an open and wonderful 'may', a 'may' which can exist even when a couple have been married for many years, a 'may' which is a celebration of the existence of the beloved partner who makes it possible not to be alone, who enriches your life and gives it meaning.

Every morning Hermione brings little Bernard to play-group, then goes home and reads the paper. Then she starts the housework, usually with something relatively unimportant. Before long she starts to feel that she is wasting her time, time which could be much better spent doing other and more important things. Shortly before she has to collect Bernard from his playgroup, she starts to feel angry that the freest part of the day is over, that she now has to hurry to get done all the things she would much rather do in a more leisurely way, and that if she doesn't do them now it will be much harder when Bernard is also demanding her attention.

Hermione too will continue to make life difficult for herself as long as she experiences her son, the housework, and everything else in her life as a 'must' in the guise of a whip which is constantly being cracked at her.

Bridget is overweight and ashamed of it, but she can never manage to diet successfully. Again and again she tries to change her eating patterns, tries this system today and another tomorrow, looks out avidly for new dietary regimes. She knows that there is a constant inner struggle in which she feels continually defeated.

Many people today are in Bridget's situation. The first step which is necessary is to admit that we do not *have* to lose weight. Being fat is a valid choice. I don't have to change my habits, and I don't have to give up eating all those tempting foods. I can also decide not to get angry when my husband comments on my figure, seeing his remarks as a well-meaning but unpsychological attempt to help, though it may well be a rewarding goal to be able to please him more. The next steps depend on Bridget's situation. Is her constant nibbling a reaction to her relationship with her husband, or was it already there when she was a child? In cases like this it may often be appropriate to seek professional psychological help. Basically, however, Bridget can also be helped by recognising which of the four basic goals she is pursuing with her compulsive eating.

21

BELIEVE INSTEAD OF HOPE

*'Pass beyond the baser stages of doubt
and rise to the exalted heights of certainty.'*[48]

In Chapter 3 we spoke about faith, that strongest of human powers, and the most important quality for social relations. Because we have not yet sufficiently recognised the existence and the importance of faith, and because believing is usually equated with having an opinion, making an assumption, or as a religious concept, we make far too little use of this power at the conscious level.

When something needs doing, or when we have a problem to solve, we usually say 'I hope I'll manage it' rather than 'I'll manage it'. Hoping, however, is not enough, because to hope means not to believe sufficiently, it means to doubt. In the sense that we are using the word, believing means to have certainty, and nothing other than belief can give us the feeling of certainty. Even knowledge only ever leads to more knowledge, never to the feeling of certainty. As long as we only hope, we express our doubt.

Mr Briggs, a married man with children, loved another woman for a long time, but he chose to decide between one woman and the other, and elected in favour of his family. Although they have made a great effort to put the whole thing in the past, there is still a shadow over the marriage which makes Mrs Briggs very unhappy. Her husband says that he cannot free himself of the other woman, but he nonetheless loves his wife very much, and would not like to relinquish her to another man. Although Mrs Briggs will not admit it to anyone, she is desperate.

Mrs Briggs has always hoped that her husband would forget the other woman and make her the only woman in his life again. But she does not believe this will happen. Why? She believes too little in her husband, and not at all in herself. How could she ever completely trust him again, she asks herself, after he has disillusioned her so much? But in thinking this way, she fails to escape the past just as surely as he does. Why? Because despite all her suffering, her husband's indiscretion gave her a feeling of moral superiority which she is not prepared to let go of. She must believe in their future together. She could, for instance, start placing more trust in her husband. As long as she only hopes, she continues to nourish her disillusionment. If, however, she did everything possible to win back her husband completely, the only path would be that of unconditional trust, without even thinking about the possibility of further failure and disappointment.

A businessman who wants to make a profit from selling something must first be prepared to invest — he must purchase the goods. Mr Briggs isn't making it easy for his wife to learn to trust him again, otherwise he wouldn't be saying things like 'he wouldn't like to relinquish her to another man' — behind this is concealed the authoritarian male belief that a woman is her husband's possession. Mr Briggs' attitude is discouraging his wife, and he doesn't help the situation by implying that his moral lapse was because his wife somehow fares badly in comparison with the other woman. On the other hand, Mrs Briggs must learn to believe more in herself, to see her positive qualities and accept her negative ones. If she believed more in her own value, her husband would in turn learn to recognise her value. The main way of doing this is by self-encouragement, and the chief means of self-encouragement is to have a positive attitude about oneself as well as about other people and the world in general. 'Whether ignorant, childish or sick, they must be loved and helped, and not disliked because of their imperfection.'[49]

If Mrs Briggs truly wants to achieve unity in her marriage, then she must help her husband. To help, however, does not mean to want to educate. She can regard him as ignorant, or as childishly immature, or as ill, as long as she does not misuse this way of seeing things and thereby feel superior to him. If he is ignorant, then she can help him gain more knowledge rather than getting angry at him. If he is childishly immature, she should help him develop from the child within the man to his full human and spiritual stature. If he is ill — and by this I mean emotionally ill — then she should help him to become healthier rather than be annoyed by his neurotic behaviour.

But she cannot see the situation in any of these ways unless she believes that her husband is capable of developing and learning, and that she can help him in this process.

22

UNDERSTAND YOUNG PEOPLE

*'Let it never be imagined that youth must await their
years of maturity before they can
render invaluable services.'*[50]

Here are some young people's own stories:

'When my brother and I wanted to go out in the evening
there was always a scene. First my father would either
say no on principle, or he would tell us to be home at an
impossible time. This usually ended up in a hopeless
discussion, with my mother just sitting there silently. If
she did join in the conversation, it often resulted in a
more acceptable compromise.'

'I didn't have a happy childhood. I lived with my parents
in an ugly rented flat. When I went home for my lunch
my father was there, and we ate our lunch together. I
always had the feeling that my father got irritable whenever I was happy. He would complain a lot, and sometimes there would be a quarrel. At weekends my father
went for long walks in the woods and always dragged me
and my mother along too. I was always very bored, and
longed to have a friend. In the evening we just sat in front
of the television. I was never really happy.'

111

'If my brother or I ever got bad marks, my mother was angry and started scolding us. That depressed us, so that when my father got home from work he immediately noticed that something was wrong. My mother blamed us for not working harder, and for having our minds on other things. My father, on the other hand, hardly reacted at all. He just said that we knew how much we had to do and it was up to us. It was true — we were old enough to know what we were doing.'

These are just three accounts of people's childhoods, but even if we were to take a hundred stories they would amount to much the same overall impression — the two generations simply do not understand each other. Young people live in the future, old people in the past, and they both tend to forget the present. On top of this is the competition that often reigns in families, and this lack of harmony effects everyone, both young and old. The older generation tries to bring up children in ways which are out of step with the times we live in, and constantly feel that they are failing. People get disheartened and fearful of each other, young people demand more freedom, and the older generation will not give up its privileges. The pressure increases, until defiance and rebellion are an everyday occurrence; it matters little whether young people rebel openly or under the surface. The young people who do not feel understood or supported seek the approval of their peers, and united in their rebellion, they then seek every effective method of exposing the impotence of the older generation — disorderliness, fantastic hair styles, loud music, smoking, alcohol, sex, drugs, and a total rejection of their parents' values.

Only when parents learn to see their children differently, to show them respect from an early age, to treat them as friends and equals, to let them contribute and to give them responsibility, to *believe* in them, will we begin to see harmony, mutual respect, love and appreciation between the generations.

There are many parents who are unwilling to recognise this, who are not prepared to see the signs of the times, for whom all these 'new' ideas are too uncomfortable, who above all are not willing to let go of the privileges they have so far enjoyed. But even in these cases there is no cause for pessimism, since even if efforts to create a better understanding and a more harmonious relationship are only made by the young, a great deal can still be achieved. The prerequisite for this to happen is that young people are encouraged to believe in themselves and in their parents' ability to change, and to take the necessary steps to achieve this. Older people can learn just as much from the young as vice versa. However, it is just as hopeless for the youth to try to 'educate' the older generation as it is for the educators to see the young only as ignorant people in need of education.

Ten rules for ending conflicts between generations
The following guidelines can help in any conflict situation, but can help particularly with difficulties between generations:

1) Accept the situation ('accept' does not imply approval!).
2) Do not try and run away from the problem.
3) Try to recognise the motives under the surface.
4) Do not develop any secret animosity.
5) Do not try to blame each other.
6) See what you can change about yourself.
7) Ask yourself what *you* can do to help the situation.
8) Forget your feelings of helplessness.
9) Do not resort to conflict or force.
10) Remember that the other person is suffering too.

These methods of behaviour can be learned and applied by both sides. It is completely idle to speculate who is more guilty. There are always two sides when the peace is disturbed. We all make mistakes, and need the courage to be imperfect. It is understandable that the young always think it is their parents who make the first mistake, but young people must come to realise that if they react in the wrong way to their parents' mistakes, they will only perpetuate them. Threat follows upon threat, revenge upon punishment, and war upon the use of force. Yet no one should let other people tell them how to behave. The young want freedom and independence, but do not realise how dependent they make themselves by their reactions and their unconscious imitation of their parents' incorrect methods. For understandable reasons, it is usually easier for the young than for adults to recognise the correct way of behaving, and to see that inner freedom, which is practically limitless, is much more important than outward freedom.

What can we do, whatever side of the conflict we find ourselves on?

1) We must accept ourselves, the young person, and the situation, renouncing negative feelings, emotions and aggressions.
2) We must recognise the problems of the young and the reasons for their rebellion.
3) We must recognise the meaning of our own fear and discouragement.
4) We must understand the consequences of changing social values, and the resulting conflict between the generations.
5) We must respect the young as equal partners, listen to them, and help them to achieve inner freedom and learn to make their own decisions.
6) We must share responsibility with the young.
7) We must allow the young to contribute and give them recognition and status, since all groups, whether of the family or school class, in work or in leisure, exhibit a

value-forming power, and can therefore help them develop their own values.

8) We can form family councils, pupil councils and student councils, but not in such a way that they are led by adults who have not been chosen by the group members. The young should also participate in community affairs, because we can always learn from the young, with their courage and enthusiasm. One example of this comes from Jacksonville in Florida, where juvenile delinquency halved after the introduction of a juvenile jury. The jury had no legal authority, but it had an important psychological effect, and the youthful jurors, having a better understanding of their peers, were better and quicker at recognising what was going on, were sharp observers, considered their verdicts carefully, and were remarkably fair.

9) We can recognise that dialogue and communication with young people in their own surroundings is often more important than the provision of leisure centres, educational establishments, counselling and therapy.

23

UNDERSTAND SEX

'Humanity is like a bird with two wings — the one is male, the other female. Unless both wings are strong and impelled by some common force, the bird cannot fly heavenward. According to the spirit of this age, women must advance and fulfil their mission in all departments of life, becoming equal to men. They must be on the same level as men and enjoy equal rights.'[51]

In the last chapter we divided people into two groups according to their age. The subject of this chapter is also two groups, but this time they are divided according to sex. It is astounding that prejudices still prevail which frequently pass as scientific facts, and it is particularly amazing that this should be the case in an age which considers itself enlightened in sexual matters. As long as the scientific method with its careful counting, weighing, measuring and experimenting holds sway, as long as materialism has the upper hand, as long as people are thought of as animals rather than as human beings with mental and spiritual qualities, then so long will physical sex continue to be overvalued. In fact the only recent development is that the overemphasis on physical sex now occurs in the open, where before it used to be hidden beneath the surface. The result is that we end up with sex having us, instead of us having sex.

Sexual activity today is regarded not so much as a means for the reproduction of the species, as it used to be, but as a means of gaining pleasure. Yet it is still misused over and over again in the service of personal superiority, prestige and social status. The essential function of sex, the physical and spiritual union which alone can lead to the unity of men and women, to a deep and lasting happiness, is often never considered at all.

The difficulties we see today in relationships between the sexes — in friendship, partnership and marriage — are not primarily sexual, but are of a social nature. During the centuries-old oppression of women by men, many commonly-held prejudices arose about the concepts of maleness and femaleness, prejudices which are to some extent held by almost everyone. The validity of these prejudices has only very slowly been thrown into doubt, following a growing realisation by women that they deserve recognition and social equality.

In order to understand how, even today, misinformed attitudes and child-raising methods transmit false values about sexual identity, sexual differences and sexual matters in general, I will introduce the psychological concept of 'masculine protest'. A better understanding of this phenomenon can help to make relations between the sexes less difficult and more satisfying.

From a woman's point of view, the masculine protest is her protest against the inferior rôle alloted to women — such a protest is thoroughly correct and very necessary in the context of women's liberation. The protest begins in early childhood, when a little girl realises that she is *only* a girl. Girls have to do things that boys do not have to do, and boys are allowed to do things that girls are not. On the basis of these observations, little girls develop attitudes and tactics which work to their disadvantage. Many young women fear marriage,

117

believing that marriage will condemn them to a perpetual second-rate position in relation to their husbands. On the surface they appear to do everything they can to find a man, but they always end up with the wrong one, because inwardly they are not looking for a lasting partnership at all. One common result is to fall in love with a man who is already married or committed — there is no surer way of avoiding marriage than falling in love with a Catholic priest! Not everyone goes that far, because it usually suffices to choose someone who is significantly older or younger, or of a different race or class.

When a young woman like this finds a man who would appear to measure up on all counts, she is almost certain to find something objectionable about him — the size of his nose or his income. Of the many other ways of avoiding marriage, two particularly successful techniques deserve mention: seeking the perfect partner, who of course does not exist, and lack of sympathy or love for anybody who seems like a suitable partner: 'What a pity; everything seems to be right, except . . . I don't love him.'

No two masculine protests are alike. Every girl develops different tactics, even if the differences are less than they may seem at first. A young woman who does not want to avoid marriage may strive for superiority in marriage, for instance by seeking a weak partner, or someone younger, or someone less educated than she is. She could also choose a much older partner, whose superiority would be easier to accept than in someone of the same age.

A man's 'masculine protest' happens in a slightly different way — in childhood he grows up with the prejudice that being male means being superior. If he allows himself to be discouraged by members of his family, he can come to believe that he is not a real man, and develop a real fear of marriage. He thinks that as a man he must play a superior rôle, but is not confident of being able to do so. In order to

118

avoid this disgrace, he will refuse to choose a woman and get married, and he will employ methods similar to those we have seen adopted by women. He will search for the perfect woman, wanting to be certain he has found 'the right one', or he will choose somebody who will submit to him totally. Or he may, as many girls do, choose very early in his life to be interested only in his own sex.

'The world in the past has been ruled by force, and man has dominated over woman by reason of his more forceful and aggressive qualities, both of body and mind. But the balance is already shifting; force is losing its dominance, and mental alertness, intuition, and the spiritual qualities of love and service, in which woman is strong, are gaining ascendancy. Hence the new age will be an age less masculine and more permeated with the feminine ideals, or, to speak more exactly, will be an age in which the masculine and feminine elements of civilisation will be more evenly balanced.'[52]

What is especially needed in order to achieve more peace and harmony in relations between the sexes is to increase women's self-confidence. As long as successful women — be it in politics, administration or industry — still consider it necessary to imitate male behaviour, it shows that not even these women believe sufficiently in the position and value of women.

A teacher told me how she had worked at a school in which the headmistress had to supervise everything that the teachers were doing, then admonished her staff and refused to listen to their suggestions. 'Eventually I couldn't stand it,' she said. 'I got myself transferred from this school, but not to the neighbouring school. That school, too, had a headmistress in charge, and the atmosphere there was reported to be very tense. I have the impression that most women in positions of authority want to fulfil their duties better than their male colleagues, an attitude which creates a tense atmosphere. I could tolerate it for a while, but I started feeling ill and tired, and always had to be punctual. Now I work under a headmaster, and the atmosphere is far more relaxed.'

This story shows that women sometimes have a very critical attitude towards successful colleagues of their own sex, another important aspect of the contemporary situation to be taken into account. In itself it is senseless to compare men with women, but sometimes it can help to strengthen a woman's feelings of her own self-worth if she can be aware that there are some important ways in which the average woman is superior to the average man in this day and age.

Women as agents of spiritual development
What has long been evident in the USA is now becoming apparent elsewhere, that it is predominantly women who sustain cultural life. Adult education courses are attended chiefly by women. The proportion of women teachers is constantly rising — and teachers are a very important force in civilisation. The number of female psychologists is rising too. It is often a woman who would rather attend a concert or a lecture in the evening, or read a book — for many men the newspaper and the television will suffice. At the same time, many men will stress just how much they have had to accomplish during the day in order to earn the daily bread.

As the last two chapters of this book will show, spiritual activity is a vitally important part of learning to relate to others.

Intuition
Even today many people regard this important human function as unscientific. This is understandable, since science in its present state cannot use its techniques to examine spiritual matters.

Intuition means inner vision — immediate, unreflected, total perception. Men often recognise that women frequently have more intuition than they do, but they do so in a very derogatory way: 'You women and your intuition! It would be better if you thought logically!'

In an age which stands on the threshold of the rediscovery of the spiritual, the recognition of women's intuition is becoming more and more significant. It also contributes to the fact that a woman, understanding reality better, is often more practical in her observations than a man, who with his ideas and theories often operates on a subjective level. Intuition is foreign to him, which can lead to a complete misunderstanding of the real facts.

Love
Like walking or talking, love must be learned. As a rule, people today have not learned how to love sufficiently. 'Love is a light that never dwelleth in a heart possessed by fear.'[53] Hearts possessed by fear are very much in evidence today, because, astonishingly, our educational methods still entail the constant discouragement of our children. Even maternal love, so highly praised, often has little in common with real love, since every mother that pampers her child is, in the final analysis, self-oriented rather than interested in helping her child.[8] Much else which today goes under the name of love — sexuality, for instance — has nothing to do with real love. Love means putting the other person first, giving all one has and is. To love is more important than to be loved.

As a rule, women are better able to love than men. They have learned better to give themselves completely. Devotion by instalments always leads to only part of the experience of real love.

Service

Service is very much out of fashion these days. Servants, maids and valets are virtually non-existent. If we need to be serviced by other people, we usually import immigrant workers. Despite this, service is probably a more important function of being human than any other. Learning to serve one another can change the world.

Service does not mean slavery. The woman who is completely at the service of her family, who waits on her husband and children from morning till night and has no time for anything else, certainly does not contribute to their personal development. The distinction is important: to serve can be the highest form of love, while to wait on somebody is demeaning.

The true service of other people, this existence-for-others, has been better learned by women than by men, who still very often like to play the rôle of slave-driver.

Mr Kimble comes home from work in the evening expecting his wife to be immediately and exclusively available for him, to embrace him joyfully and lovingly, and to make a fuss over him. She, on the other hand, does not find the warrior's return from battle particularly stimulating, since he shows no respect for her at all, and has no interest whatsoever in her work.

Of course, it would be nice if Mrs Kimble were to greet her husband in the way he expects, but then he would have to change his attitude to her and her work. Love cannot be demanded, only earned. As we have seen in Chapter 10, we are always on the wrong track when we think we know what the other person should or should not do. Instead we should be asking: 'What can *I* do?'

Mr Villiers points out to his wife that he has already been wearing the same shirt for three days. She asks him why he is telling her this, and he replies that all his other shirts are dirty. Mrs Villiers suggests that he should go to the laundry room and wash them. 'But that's your job!' says her husband. Now the Villiers are a young married couple who agreed, as long as they did not have any children, that both of them would work and both share whatever housework needed to be done in the evenings. But . . .?

Half measures solve nothing

As long as we give only half of ourselves, there is always the danger that we can come to believe that we are giving 51% and receiving only 49%. In a lifelong partnership, a marriage, it is only meaningful if each person contributes 100%, giving totally on every level — physical, emotional and spiritual. It only works if we can put our interests completely in our partner's hands, loving him or her unconditionally, wanting to serve him or her from beginning to end.

Mrs Richardson has been cleaning up the kitchen for more than an hour. When her husband comes in he says, 'What are you still doing in here?' She reacts irritably, and when he asks what is wrong, she says, 'I'm not the servant, you know.' Mr Richardson moves onto the defensive. 'Come on,' he says, 'I do my share. I just do different things, like we agreed. I really don't do less than you do.' He feels unfairly treated, and wants to tell her all the things that he does every day without even mentioning them. Inwardly he endures her lack of objectivity; outwardly he makes an effort to speak gently and carefully, and he leaves the kitchen quietly. But the anger is still there in his stomach. He is angry that this situation keeps happening, even though she must realise that what she says doesn't fit with the facts.

When someone notices that their partner is in a bad mood, the question 'What's wrong?' is not only unnecessary, but is likely to be the prelude to a fight. At times like this it is far better to think what I can do myself. Can I show my sympathy? Can I encourage them? Can I help them with what they are doing? Perhaps all they need is to be left alone for a while so they can think about what has happened. In these ways we can demonstrate a positive attitude towards our partner, a trust, a belief in them, a belief that they will be able to cope with the situation. Mr Richardson must learn to put love before justice, and not to misuse his sense of justice so that he can feel more fair than his wife, and thus achieve a feeling of superiority.

Maria's father will simply not understand that choosing a profession is important for girls too. He regards her as an ideal help for her mother, and perhaps later she might do something like dressmaking, which would be a useful thing for a housewife to know. Maria, however, has had quite enough of housework, and she lets her father know what she thinks about his plans in no uncertain terms. She tells him what she thinks about women's inferior status in the world, though she knows very well that he reacts strongly and emotionally whenever she mentions the subject.

These last two examples are typical of the way in which men still clearly do not respect women. They show this in a multitude of ways, talking about politics and business in the hope that women will not be able to keep up, devoting themselves to 'male' hobbies and sports, and so on.

Roddy and Emma are out walking. Every time they pass a woman, Roddy insists on making remarks about her, things like 'She's a dead loss!' or 'Wouldn't mind having her for a night.' Eventually Emma has had enough.

'Your comments make me feel sick!' she says. Roddy is quite visibly shocked, since he didn't mean any harm by his remarks. He tries to justify himself, to explain that he didn't really mean it. That just makes things worse.

The fact that Emma is annoyed by Roddy's behaviour, though incorrect, is completely understandable. In acting the way he is, he is expressing his disdain for her and for women in general.

When Conrad finds himself alone in the evening, especially at weekends, he will ring up one of a number of girls he is friends with to arrange to go for a walk or go to the cinema. The girl he rings will usually already have something planned, so declines Conrad's offer. He stays friendly and tries hard not to show his disappointment, but when he has put the phone down he feels very lonely and dissatisfied. He gets angry with himself, and tends to blame the girl who has refused his invitation.

Conrad, too, has little respect for women. 'Okay,' he is saying, 'here I am! All I need to do is give the sign, and everyone should be at my disposal.' This is asking a great deal. Does Conrad really think that everyone is waiting for him, or does he secretly have an investment in being rejected? Is this his variety of 'masculine protest'?

Tanya has been engaged for nearly a year, but she is concerned about the relationship because her fiancé feels trapped by the engagement. He would still like to be as free as he was before to make approaches to every woman he likes. He thinks that this is his right, and that Tanya has no reason to object. But Tanya feels that she is in constant competition with other women, and cannot freely and openly express her feelings about his behaviour.

Why does Tanya remain with this man? Is she afraid of losing him and not finding anyone else? This is no basis for a relationship between equals. If she thought about it, she would realise that even after the wedding he, as a man, would demand special privileges, and not feel that he had to take the question of fidelity too seriously. It would be much better for her to discuss all this with her fiancé, and make it clear in a firm but friendly way that the situation is untenable. She loves him and would like to stay with him, but not under these degrading conditions. The decision is now in his hands.

Jealousy

Mrs Sharpe is fearfully jealous of everything and anything. If Mr Sharpe comes home five minutes later than usual she makes a dreadful scene. He naturally justifies and defends himself, which only makes her more suspicious, so again and again they are at loggerheads.

Jealousy is one of the most common of emotions, but it has nothing to do with love, as is so often supposed. Jealousy is a hostile feeling which surfaces most often when our self-confidence is at a low ebb. Do I still have enough to offer my partner, or are other people offering him or her more? Mrs Sharpe is five years older than her husband, and it may be that this makes her feel inferior; her goal is thus to show herself to be superior. We can recognise this goal from the subject of the argument, which is supposed to result in Mr Sharpe coming home five minutes earlier. Of course, it is possible to use jealousy to pursue any of the four goals of Chapter 2.

Mr Sharpe makes the mistake of justifying himself, even though there is nothing whatsoever in the claim of infidelity. In order to help his wife he could instead greet her with a loving smile, a tender kiss, or any other sign of his real affection. He must not let himself be drawn into a quarrel, recognising that it is not he who is suffering, but his wife who needs help and encouragement.

Sexual incompatibility

Incompatibility in sexual matters is another problem which originates in a lack of understanding about sex. When sexual relations between a man and a woman are not good, it seems that either the man 'can't' — he is impotent — or the woman is incapable of responding and is emotionally cold — she is frigid. For those who do not see or want to admit to the personal conflicts which lie behind these 'conditions', the label of 'sexual incompatibility' between two partners has proved very convenient. I doubt very much whether there is really such a thing as sexual incompatibility at all, as long as two partners accept each other, are mutually suited, leave their egos behind, form a confident, trusting and positive attitude towards each other, and recognise that any initial delayed reaction on either part is probably of social origin.

Almost all the initial difficulties can be overcome if the sexual dimension of a partnership is not overvalued, creating a feeling of obligation (and many men still think that sexual potency is the best sign of masculinity!). Instead, sex should be regarded primarily as a means of union which can lead to unity between a man and a woman. Sex, like love, must be learned, and should be regarded as a training in partnership, for which neither person bears more responsibility than the other. Frank and open communication about everything each partner likes or does not like can be of great assistance. If the partners believe themselves to be incapable of such communication, they should not hesitate to seek professional advice. Sexual incompatibility is not the cause of impotence and frigidity — it is the result of personal conflict and insufficient cooperation (see Chapter 13).

In-laws — a shared responsibility

Relationships with in-laws frequently create problems within a marriage. If the following guidelines are observed, however, most difficulties with in-laws can be solved.

1) The in-laws should be regarded as the partners' joint responsibility.
2) One partner should never criticise an in-law unilaterally.
3) The partners must learn to agree on issues connected with their in-laws.
4) The unity between the partners should exist both inwardly and outwardly.

The most difficult situations arise when circumstances require one or more of the in-laws to live with a married couple. If this really cannot be avoided, we must keep in mind that the most important means of establishing unity is dialogue (Chapter 9). Also essential is the recognition that the person who is most obviously suffering is not always the one who is suffering most. If, for example, the husband's mother lives with a couple and does not get on well with her daughter-in-law, it is very often the husband and not the wife who bears the greater suffering. Even though it may at first seem otherwise, he has a difficult choice to make. He wants to be on good terms with his wife as well as with his mother, and does not want to hurt anyone. If, however, taking sides is unavoidable, he should always side with his wife, since unity between husband and wife is essential.

Here are some further suggestions for establishing greater unity:

— Adopt the right attitude to each other.
— Accommodate each other, but not at any price.
— Be polite.
— Agree, but do not make contracts with each other.
— Obtain your partner's consent, but do not demand it.

- Be willing to encourage your partner.
- Remember to keep working at loving your partner.
- Deal with problems together.
- Always try to think what *you* can do to help.

24

COME TO GRIPS
WITH LIFE'S TASKS

*'The essence of faith is fewness of words
and abundance of deeds.'*[55]

What I see as the tasks of life are the following (for more detailed information, see my book on self-education[1]):

1) Life's work, occupation or profession.
2) Love and marriage.
3) Communion with nature and the material world, other people, art and science, myself, and the spiritual dimension.

To be fully human means at least coming to grips with, if not solving, all of life's tasks. We should not completely neglect any of them, or play them off against each other. We should concentrate on each one as well as all the others.

Mr and Mrs Edwards have been married for five years and have two children. Their marriage is not going well, and they are on the verge of thinking about a divorce. Mr Edwards is busy building up a business, and has no time at all for his family. The result is an endless power struggle with his wife. He never comes home when he says he is going to, even if he has phoned from work a short while beforehand. Mrs Edwards feels that he couldn't care less about his family, and doesn't want to listen to her problems. She feels utterly neglected by her husband, and consequently has virtually stopped being interested in him and his business problems.

It is true that it takes a long time to build up a successful new business. To begin with Mrs Edwards was with her husband all the way; she helped him, and believed him when he said that things would soon get better. In fact things just became worse and worse, and eventually Mrs Edwards lost faith in her husband completely. She took to tactics of petty revenge, but these, of course, just made things worse. Without going into more details, it is very clear that Mr Edwards is misusing the task of setting up his life's work in order to evade his responsibility for his other life's tasks, notably love and marriage.

Mr Atkinson idolises his wife and does everything for her. In the morning he makes breakfast for her so she can stay in bed longer. He takes care of the two little children, washes them, dresses them, plays and talks with them. When the time comes to go shopping, his wife gets up. He comes home with ideas for lunch, which he cooks, of course, though he never forgets to bring home a little something for his wife — flowers or sweets. After lunch she lies down again while he attends to his business with typewriter and telephone. Mrs Atkinson never needs to worry about anything, never has to make a decision, has time for her children, and lets her husband wait on the family. It all works wonderfully. She is still very young, and regards her husband with admiration. Sometimes she longs to go out in the evening instead of sitting in front of the colour television, and he willingly takes her out for dinner, or to the cinema or theatre. An ideal family life?

He often tells her about his grandiose business plans and his successes. One day, however, they have to move house quite suddenly, and move to another city. He explains to her that the move is necessary because of 'evil people' and 'society in general'. They move so quickly that they have to leave a lot behind, but everything needed for the new house is soon bought anew.

It isn't long before Mr Atkinson tells his wife that they are going to have to move again — other people are again to blame. The departure was very rapid, and Mrs Atkinson was unable to take even the essentials. They were hardly settled into their new house when the police called, and took Mr Atkinson away. Mrs Atkinson's world collapsed about her. After some time, and talking to a lot of people, she discovered that her husband had never been as successful as he claimed, and had been living at other people's expense. He was a master at obtaining credit. He went to prison, and Mrs Atkinson and her children had to face the real world.

On the face of it, Mr Atkinson was the perfect paterfamilias. It is a shame he was not aware of all his life's tasks and the need to come to grips with everything. We cannot live in society and completely disregard its accepted rules of social conduct. Even if the rules and laws of the society we live in sometimes appear to be incorrect, it is even more incorrect simply to ignore them. Our task consists first of following the laws, but then in using our knowledge to help society recognise whatever is incorrect, and take steps to improve it.

Alexander is happy. He has finally found people by whom he feels completely accepted. Without criticising him or saying negative things about his lifestyle, they simply love him as a fellow human being. They all belong to a religious association, and Alexander becomes so enthusiastic that he wants to devote himself completely to this new-found cause. As a result he has not been too bothered about completing his college course or finding a job. Fortunately his new friends are very understanding, and help him lovingly towards a more positive attitude to learning and working.

Alexander was fortunate in finding friends who did not let him misuse the task of exploring the spiritual dimension — in this case religion — at the expense of the task of his life's work.

Mr and Mrs Tuttle are wonderful people, hard-working, committed, educated and spiritually advanced. Their children, a daughter and a son, are their parents' joy. A sense of unity pervades the family, and whatever needs doing is done jointly. Only rarely is one member of the family seen without the others. Mr and Mrs Tuttle only really have one problem: they cannot understand why neither of their children has been able to decide on a partner. After all, they would both be extremely desirable partners.

Each member of the Tuttle family, even though they would hardly admit it, feels that they are particularly special. The quality of their family life is very high, and so are their standards and ambitions. It is virtually impossible for any outsider to live up to the standards they set. The search for a suitable — well-nigh perfect — partner is the perfect alibi for avoiding their life's task of marriage.

Olaf lives completely for his art. He has already made something of a name for himself as a painter, but he also likes writing and music. In his private life he takes pains to give the air of a genius who deserves everyone's admiration. His wife is very unhappy, partly because they have constant financial problems, but also because Olaf is a useless organiser. As an artist he needs 'freedom', meaning that nobody has the right to bother him with everyday trivialities, to hem him in, or to make any demands on him at all. The rules he makes for his relationships are to be observed by the other people, not him. He comes and goes when he pleases, demands to have his meals exactly when it suits him, turns night into day and vice versa, leaves a mess in his wake everywhere he goes, and 'naturally' keeps a mistress, a girl who worships him.

Olaf isn't the only one — there are many artists like Olaf who capitalise on their art to satisfy their need for personal recognition. But artists too must learn to live with other people, and although it needs courage and sensitivity, this can be done without any risk to their artistic capabilities and creative powers. Artists who can recognise the need to fulfil all of life's tasks believe in life, in creation, in themselves and in other people, and have no need for ruses which involve them living at the expense of others.

Mrs Clarke is crazy about animals. There isn't a room in her flat which isn't occupied by animals, even if it is only a temporary haven for an animal that is sick or in need of special care. Even she doesn't know how many birds she has — birds are her special interest, and she has written a book on them — but there are also dogs and cats, mice and fish. She goes to as many pet shows as she can.

This interest in animals means that she has little time for her husband, apart from asking him to help her with her animals. Eventually Mr Clarke feels that he is actually married to the animals rather than to his wife, it comes to a separation, and he moves out.

An exaggerated interest in nature often indicates that a person has had bad experiences with other people, usually with their own mother, in their childhood. The feeling that

134

they cannot trust other people, or that other people are unjust and cruel, leads many children to turn to nature and animals, since they cannot be let down by animals in the same way. It must be stressed that these early experiences need not correspond with the facts, and may not be remembered — Mrs Clarke, for example, may only remember good things about her childhood.

I could give countless examples of the misuse of our life's tasks. There is the businessman who is married to two wives. Officially he is only married to one, but the other too shares a house and children with him. He seems to be the perfect father to both households; they know about each other, and the children all seem to get on well, but the two women are not happy . . .

Or there is the enchanting couple, devoted to spiritual things, and incredibly loving to each other. Everybody considers them to be very happy. But something is wrong — here it is in the sexual dimension. They experienced some problems in this area of their relationship early on in the marriage, but instead of working together to solve them, they have ended up in a trap where there is no sex at all in their partnership. Yet this dimension is indispensable if complete unity with the loved partner is to be achieved.

Our communion with ourselves is probably the task neglected by most people today, the one least recognised in a positive light. This is why I mention so often the importance of self-education.

Hospitality
'Do not be content with showing friendship in words alone.'[56]
True hospitality, even towards a stranger, is a virtue which we practise less and less. It provides a wonderful opportunity to fulfil the task of communion with other people. We often think we don't have the time to be hospitable, and we

always have good excuses at hand, excuses like not feeling comfortable with a potential guest.

Moderation

'The civilisation, so often vaunted . . . will, if allowed to overleap the bounds of moderation, bring great evil upon men.'[57]

We have seen from the preceding examples what difficulties can arise from the exaggeration of just one of our life's tasks. Every exaggeration is incorrect. All the 'isms' of our times are such exaggerations: egoism, materialism, hedonism, intellectualism and so on. We can misuse anything, and exaggeration is always a misuse, even when it involves the most positive things. Exaggerated love leads to indulgence; exaggerated faith to superstition; exaggerated knowledge to a blind faith in science. Misuse can work on a physical plane too: someone who eats excessive amounts of food with a high nutritional value, such as milk and honey, will become ill.

Live according to a plan

Before setting out on a journey we usually look at a map and make a plan. The same should apply to the journey through life. Anyone who wants to achieve something in their life, who wants to develop their potential to the fullest, should work out a personal plan. Without a plan we shall remain indifferent, and not capitalise sufficiently on our resources. A housewife who does not plan becomes a slave to housework and her family. She works from hand to mouth, and never has time for anything else. But as soon as she makes a plan and organises her time, she becomes the mistress of her time and work, and of the household. She will suddenly find time to do other things too — to pursue a hobby, perhaps, or, depending how old her children are, to work outside the home. A job outside the home has three advantages

— she is serving the greater community, she is serving herself by developing her potential, and she is serving her family, particularly her children, for whom she becomes even more interesting by being able to impart new knowledge, information and skills.

25

LIVE MORE CONSCIOUSLY

*'True loss is for him whose days have been
spent in utter ignorance of his self.'*[58]

As we saw in Chapter 1, we make most of our decisions
unconsciously — most choices we make do not reach the
level of consciousness. Individual psychology, however,
does not interpret this as meaning that there is a power 'in
the depths' which operates independently of a person, as
other schools of psychology do. It sees the so-called 'unconscious' as part of the *whole* person, with two main func-
tions: first there is the function of economy, which ensures
that decisions do not always require our full attention, and
then there is the function of convenient forgetfulness,
which allows us to overlook inclinations and intentions
which we would prefer not to admit to ourselves, because
we want to have a good opinion of ourselves. The so-called
'depth' is only one dimension, subordinate to the view of
man as a whole and unified being.

Accepting our life's tasks can help us to live more consciously. We can and must learn the rules necessary for our
own self-education[1] and the rules for our social relations
with others, then we can bring up our children to be happier and more self-confident.[8]

If I understand and use these rules, then I am no longer

the slave of my moods, states of mind, emotions and aggressions, negative feelings and expressions of hostility. I am their master. At the same time I am no longer dependent upon other people's opinions, understandings and judgements, but relatively free to direct my life, my behaviour, my actions, thoughts and feelings, according to objective values, such as concern for others and the fear of God. Perhaps I will not always be able to do what I consider to be right — circumstances and other people may be powerful enough to prevent me from doing that — but nothing and no one can stop me *wanting* to do whatever it is that I recognise as right.

Applying the principles
Once we have adopted a clear philosophy of life, and acknowledged the principles, rules and suggestions necessary to follow this philosophy, then we should have no problem working out which principle should have precedence in any given situation.

Mr and Mrs Harrison are modern young people who subscribe to the principle of equal rights for men and women, of mutual freedom and independence. They have rightly recognised that in a partnership it is wrong for one of the partners to make rules for the other.

Not long after the birth of their little daughter, their first child, Mrs Harrison made the acquaintance of a young man and wanted to go to bed with him. She talked about her desire with her husband, and because he wanted to uphold their ideals of freedom and equality and show how magnanimous he was, he permitted her this freedom. Not long afterwards, he acquired a girl-friend.

Mrs Harrison enjoyed her new freedom, and started to float from one lover to another. It was almost as though she was collecting men, and even when she brought a new lover home or went on holiday with him, Mr Harrison acquiesced, even though he suffered more than he would admit to himself.

Was Mrs Harrison happy? After a year or so she and her husband were talking about separating. Even though they both still believed in mutual support, and even though they were both suffering, they did not really start to tackle what was going on until they jointly sought professional help.

The Harrisons rightly wanted to avoid a situation where one of them controlled the other's life, but they were not yet aware enough to recognise that besides outward freedom there is another and more important kind of freedom — the inner freedom which exists on the spiritual plane. The bond between two people in a partnership always requires that outward material freedom be limited, but inner freedom is unlimited. I can do what I want, but I avoid doing the things I know my partner does not like. This is not a compulsion for me, however. I freely choose to take my partner into account, out of thankfulness for his or her existence and for our mutual happiness. This renunciation is no 'must', but a 'may' which makes us both happy. Mr and Mrs Harrison had also not recognised that in this case another principle had priority — the striving of each person, unconscious though it may be, to feel a sense of belonging, to form a unity with the loved partner, to forget the 'I' in favour of the 'we'.

Another important principle, as we have already seen, is the observance of the rules of the society we live in. It is precisely these rules (in this case that of monogamy) which are not accepted by many 'freedom'-loving individualists. They are convinced that they are progressive, yet they stand in the way of progress because of their lack of deep consciousness.

It is as impossible to be 'just a little married' as it is to be 'just a little pregnant'. A partnership only becomes authentic if each person is involved 100%. And how do we recognise what is authentic? From the mutual happiness we find in being with each other. Mr and Mrs Harrison found a short-lived satisfaction over and over again, but at the deepest level they were both unhappy, because to give yourself to each other only by instalments cannot lead to lasting happiness. And what makes things difficult in our time is that so few people still believe in the possibility of permanence, of lasting happiness in a partnership.

Thirty people were on a course together, and the fact that some were smokers and some were not was constantly causing problems. The non-smokers asked the smokers to regulate their smoking, and to begin with the smokers irritably refused their request. 'We won't let anybody dictate to us. After all, we're not dictating to you!' Many different compromises were attempted, but every effort to limit smoking to certain times and places failed completely, because individual smokers 'forgot' the agreement, and the non-smokers grew tired of constantly reminding them. It sometimes felt as though it was the non-smokers who were the trouble-makers.

The smokers' objection that they shouldn't let anybody dictate to them is absolutely illogical, since if they smoke it is they who are dictating that others must breathe in the air they have polluted. It is as if someone spits at another, then says: 'You mustn't object, because then there will be a quarrel, which we both want to avoid.'

Smokers who behave in this way are inconsiderate and egotistic, thinking only of their 'rights' without having sufficient sense of social responsibility to think of the rights of others.

The principle of the right to breathe clean air takes

precedence over the principle of the right to personal pleasure, since the air in a space which is used by a community is communal property.

26

BECOME MORE SPIRITUAL

'Man is, in reality, a spiritual being, and only when he lives in the spirit is he truly happy.'[59]

Spiritualisation is the way from egotism to spirituality. It is therefore very important that we develop on the spiritual level as well as on the physical and psychological planes. We have seen how we cannot and should not try to eliminate our ego completely as long as we live on the material plane, for that would indicate perfection, which cannot ever be attained, but which we should hold up as a goal towards which we can direct our lives.

Everyone longs for spirituality, even though they may not recognise it, for spirituality is the essential means for making real love possible, for giving meaning to our lives, and helping us to solve our problems. True consciousness must always be a spiritual consciousness too. It is really the spiritual dimension which makes us human, which is the essence of humanity. Only the spirit allows us to overcome troubles, cares, sorrows, pain, suffering and passion, regardless of what our body and mind have to go through. True love is always a spiritual love, making love for humanity possible. Without this spiritual orientation there can be no real understanding of each other, and our relations with other people will not lead to the happiness we look for.

We do not know everything that constitutes the spiritual realm. We only know that it is free from the earthly categories of space and time. We know something of spiritual manifestations such as intuition, dreams and anticipation, but the spiritual dimension evades examination whenever we try to comprehend it using scientific methods. We will never be able to understand it completely, because spirituality is what embraces and encompasses us. We are as little able to comprehend it as the bread can comprehend the baker, or paintings the painter.

Alfred Adler, the founder of individual psychology, and Rudolf Dreikurs who further developed it, both made an effort to comprehend this new understanding of the spiritual plane. 'Man knows much more than he understands' is the quotation that Adler placed at the head of his last and most important work, *The Meaning of Life*. Dreikurs said: 'In sexual love it is not the technique but the spirit which counts,' and: 'One can only encourage a child when one believes in that child as he is.'

Today we need no longer shrink from including the spiritual in our conscious thinking and experience, since not only has psychology embraced it as the most important thing in human existence, but the natural sciences such as physics are also coming to accept its importance. Several decades ago Professor Planck said that matter *per se* does not exist; it only arises and continues to exist through a power behind it which we must suppose is a conscious, intelligent spirit, the primeval basis of all matter. A.S. Eddington is convinced that the basis of everything is of a spiritual nature, and W. Heitler believes that we cannot escape the conclusion 'that even outside us something spiritual exists, a spiritual principle, which is connected with the laws and events of the material world as well as with our spiritual activity.'[60]

In the January 1958 issue of *The Communist*, the

Kremlin's journal, we read: 'A bitter struggle between materialism and idealism has arisen over the nature of the forces in the atomic nucleus . . . Some scientists even maintain that it is time for us to be able to achieve coexistence between the two. This, however, is the ideological disarmament of Soviet science.' As we know, Marxist-Leninist philosophy is based on materialism, so the acknowledgement of a spiritual principle would mean that this philosophy is false.

If we strive to become more spiritual, we cannot escape the concept of 'God'. Can we know God? If we mean to understand his essentially unknowable essence, of course not. But we can come to know Him in the same way that people have done for millennia, namely through those who reveal Him, His manifestations, prophets and messengers such as Abraham and Krishna, Moses, Zoroaster and Buddha, Jesus Christ, Mohammed, the Báb and Bahá'u'-lláh.

They all brought to the people of their time a new message from God, a message which taught love of God and one's fellow human beings, combined with rules and principles designed to develop and enhance social life, according to their powers of comprehension and the state of their development.

What matters is the spiritual transformation of the individual

'To man is given the special gift of the intellect . . .'[61] Our social relationships are not improved by government laws and decrees — someone has calculated that today we need thirty million laws to do justice to the ten commandments of Moses — nor by economic theories, which are often seen as a universal remedy for all ills. None of these measures has yet succeeded in making social relations more peaceful and happy. On the contrary; never has there

145

been so much fear and conflict, struggle and war in the world.

The spiritual transformation of the individual seems to be the most urgent problem of our time, and the principles outlined in this book are intended to help in this process. Through the spiritual transformation of the individual, social relations become happier and more peaceful, and through better social relations the individual becomes more spiritual. This transformation has two other consequences for each individual — the refinement of feeling, thinking, believing and acting; and the radiation of inner peace and happiness.

In return, our knowledge, love and belief, our ability to understand and be understood, our ability to help, grow through refinement, and our radiation can be a help to others. Buddha once said: 'To help one individual soul is more noble than to immerse oneself for a lifetime in the secrets of this world and the next.' When I help, I am helped. We all need one another's help. To understand and be understood, to become more spiritual, to help each other through knowledge, love and belief, leads to what we are all seeking: peace and unity among all people.

THE NEW PRINCIPLES
OF EDUCATION FOR
SUCCESSFUL RELATIONSHIPS

1. Decide more consciously.
2. Decide for purer motives.
3. Believe more strongly.
4. Act, do not react.
5. Look beneath the surface.
6. Leave the past behind.
7. Neither quarrel nor give in, but understand and want to help.
8. Distinguish between the doer and the deed.
9. Talk to each other.
10. Agree despite your differences.
11. Respect each other.
12. Do not compare yourself.
13. Cooperate.
14. Look for the positive.
15. Put yourself in neutral.
16. Turn big mistakes into little ones.
17. Do not expect a reward for good deeds.
18. Do instead of try.
19. Welcome difficulties.
20. 'May' instead of 'must'.
21. Believe instead of hope.
22. Understand young people.
23. Understand sex.
24. Come to grips with life's tasks.
25. Live more consciously.
26. Become more spiritual.

THE PRINCIPLES
MENTIONED IN THE BOOK
(in order of chapters)

Chapter 1
We are decision-making beings.
Aggression is a means to an end.
Suffer injustice rather than create injustice.
We can misuse anything.
We create anger ourselves.

Chapter 2
People make themselves superior because they need to.
Humour usually helps.
We are all goal-oriented.
We know more than we understand.
Do not make other people's problems your own.
Acknowledge people's power without giving away your own.

Chapter 3
Faith is the greatest of human powers.
Believing is a human function.
Courage is faith in yourself.
Social concern is faith in other people.
Fear is a belief in something negative.

Chapter 4
We do what we can.
We pay a price for the things we do out of fear and cowardice.

Fear is also a decision.
It is useful to imagine the worst thing that can happen.
To love is more important than to be loved.
It never pays to run away from something.
Never let yourself be treated unworthily.
Be spontaneous rather than impulsive.

Chapter 5
Do not overrate facts.
Do not over-rationalise.
It is unimportant who starts the quarrel.
See the whole situation, not just your own point of view.

Chapter 6
Do not overrate causes.
Do not overrate guilt.
Feelings of guilt are harmful.
To fall is neither dangerous nor shameful; to remain lying down is both.
Adopt a more positive outlook.

Chapter 7
Conflict begets further conflict.
Conflict arises when someone who wants to be right finds someone else who wants to be right.
When someone is right and wants to be right, they are wrong no matter how right they are.
The right should serve us, not us the right.
Take the first step yourself.
Treat your partner's existence as a blessing.
You can always learn from the other person.
Think how you can encourage the other person.
Other people are fellow human beings, not competitors.
Be friendly *and* firm.
The wise person understands and helps.

Do not tilt at windmills.
To be right is not one of life's tasks.

Chapter 8
Separate the person from the deed.
Act to please, not to hurt the other person.

Chapter 9
Ask the other person for help.
Agree on a time for dialogue.
Agree on a place for dialogue.
Dialogue is not possible as long as there are negative feelings.
Reprimanding a person is always wrong.
Do not harp upon your own rights.
Be patient.
Never come to the other person with their problem, only with your own.
When negative feelings arise, adjourn the dialogue.
Do not use rules as tricks and tactics.

Chapter 10
See differences of opinion as something positive.
Everyone has a right to their own opinion.
Everyone has a right to express their opinion.
Do not think about what the other person should or should not do.

Chapter 11
All people are equal.
Relatives are people too.
Speak only positively about other people.
Each of us is a mine rich in gems.

Chapter 12
Become more objective.

Chapter 13
Fear is the main obstacle to cooperation.
Affirm the importance of the other person.
Put your interests in your partner's hands.
Courage and social concern are necessary for cooperation.

Chapter 14
A clear philosophy of life is important.
We give meaning to things, not things to us.
Cultivate a positive outlook rather than a fault-oriented one.
Deep inside we are interested in other people's mistakes.
Treat young people as friends.
Remember that optimism pays.
Duties can also be regarded as rights.

Chapter 15
Our worth does not depend on our success.

Chapter 16
To be human means to make mistakes.
Have a policy of taking small steps.

Chapter 19
Problems can be blessings in disguise.
Use difficulties properly.
Every obstacle can be a stepping stone to progress.
Every day is the most beautiful day in our lives.
Contributing makes us happy.

Chapter 21
Develop a positive outlook towards yourself too.
See if a person needs help because they are ignorant, child-
ish or ill.

Chapter 22
All generations are equal.

Allow the young to contribute.

Give the young responsibility.

Explore the use of family councils, student councils and community councils.

Explore the use of group discussions.

Chapter 23
Men and women are equal.

Sexual problems are usually social problems.

Understand the importance of the 'masculine protest'.

Remember that we are all adaptable.

The greater the knowledge, the greater the responsibility.

Put love before justice.

Remember the essential unity of men and women.

Be polite.

Strive daily for your partner's love.

Chapter 24
Remember that all our life's tasks are important.

Do not play any of your life's tasks off against the others.

Chapter 25
What matters is not 'the depths', but the whole.

The inner, not the outer, freedom is decisive.

Follow the laws of society.

Chapter 26
Perfection should be a goal, not to be reached, but to give us direction.

Spirituality is the essence of being human.

Refinement is essential.

We can learn to radiate.

NOTES

1. Erik Blumenthal, *Wege zur inneren Freiheit*. Rex Verlag, München, 1981.
2. Bahá'u'lláh, *Gleanings from the Writings of Bahá'u'lláh*, p.148. UK Bahá'í Publishing Trust, 1949.
3. 'Abdu'l-Bahá, *Some Answered Questions*, p.302. US Bahá'í Publishing Trust, 1981.
4. See note 1 above.
5. 'Abdu'l-Bahá, *Star of the West* Magazine, December 1921.
6. Erik Blumenthal, *Erkenntnis, Liebe, Glaube — Dreigestrin der Einheit*, pp.195-206, 'Engadiner Kollegium, Vom Sinn und Wert des Lebens', Editio Academia, Zürich, 1975.
7. See note 1 above for a more detailed discussion of the power of faith.
8. Rudolf Dreikurs and Erik Blumenthal, *Eltern und Kinder — Freunde oder Feinde?* Ernst-Klett Verlag, Stuttgart.
9. Bahá'u'lláh, *Gleanings*, p.143.
10. 'Abdu'l-Bahá, *Paris Talks*, p.80. UK Bahá'í Publishing Trust, 1969.
11. Shoghi Effendi, quoted in *Living the Life*, p.20. UK Bahá'í Publishing Trust, 1974.
12. Ibid., p.33.
13. See note 1 above.
14. Bahá'u'lláh, *The Hidden Words*, p.52. Oneworld Publications, England, 1986.
15. 'Abdu'l-Bahá, *The Promulgation of Universal Peace*, p.470. US Bahá'í Publishing Trust, 1982.
16. 'Abdu'l-Bahá, *Star of the West*, March 1920.
17. Bahá'u'lláh, *Tablets of Bahá'u'lláh*, p.126. Bahá'í World Centre, 1978.
18. 'Abdu'l-Bahá, *Paris Talks*, p.53.
19. 'Abdu'l-Bahá, *Selections from the Writings of 'Abdu'l-Bahá*, p.87. Bahá'í World Centre, 1978.
20. Bahá'u'lláh, *Gleanings*, p.259.
21. Ibid., p.264.
22. Ibid., p.286.
23. 'Abdu'l-Bahá, *Paris Talks*, p.53.
24. 'Abdu'l-Bahá, quoted in *The Bahá'í World*, Vol. IV, p.384. US Bahá'í Publishing Trust, 1933.

25. Bahá'u'lláh, *The Hidden Words*, p.52.
26. 'Abdu'l-Bahá, *Paris Talks*, p.16.
27. 'Abdu'l-Bahá, *Bahá'í World Faith*, p.401. US Bahá'í Publishing Trust, 1956.
28. 'Abdu'l-Bahá, quoted in *Bahá'u'lláh and the New Era* by J.E. Esslemont, p.80. UK Bahá'í Publishing Trust, 1974.
29. Bahá'u'lláh, *Gleanings*, p.81.
30. 'Abdu'l-Bahá, *The Promulgation of Universal Peace*, p.93.
31. 'Abdu'l-Bahá, *Paris Talks*, p.39.
32. Bahá'u'lláh, *Tablets of Bahá'u'lláh*, p.35.
33. Bahá'u'lláh, *Epistle to the Son of the Wolf*, p.30. US Bahá'í Publishing Trust, 1953.
34. 'Abdu'l-Bahá, *Paris Talks*, p.160.
35. Shoghi Effendi, quoted in *Living the Life*, p.17.
36. 'Abdu'l-Bahá, *Paris Talks*, p.38.
37. 'Abdu'l-Bahá, quoted in *The Divine Art of Living*, p.46. US Bahá'í Publishing Trust, 1960.
38. 'Abdu'l-Bahá, *Paris Talks*, p.16.
39. Bahá'u'lláh, *Tablets of Bahá'u'lláh*, p.24.
40. Shoghi Effendi, quoted in *Living the Life*, p.30.
41. 'Abdu'l-Bahá, *Paris Talks*, p.51.
42. Ibid., p.72.
43. See for example *Bahá'í Prayers*, p.60. UK Bahá'í Publishing Trust, 1975.
44. Shoghi Effendi, quoted in *Living the Life*, p.17.
45. Ibid., p.30.
46. Ibid., p.37.
47. 'Abdu'l-Bahá, *The Secret of Divine Civilisation*, p.54. US Bahá'í Publishing Trust, 1970.
48. Bahá'u'lláh, *The Hidden Words*, p.54.
49. 'Abdu'l-Bahá, *Paris Talks*, p.121.
50. The Universal House of Justice, *Wellspring of Guidance*, p.92. US Bahá'í Publishing Trust, 1969.
51. 'Abdu'l-Bahá, quoted in *Bahá'u'lláh and the New Era*, p.154.
52. Ibid., p.141.
53. Bahá'u'lláh, *The Seven Valleys and The Four Valleys*, p.55. US Bahá'í Publishing Trust, 1978.
54. Rudolf Dreikurs, *Die Ehe — eine Herausforderung*, Ernst-Klett Verlag, Stuttgart.

55. Bahá'u'lláh, *Tablets of Bahá'u'lláh*, p.156.
56. 'Abdu'l-Bahá, *Paris Talks*, p.16.
57. Bahá'u'lláh, *Gleanings*, p.341.
58. Bahá'u'lláh, *Tablets of Bahá'u'lláh*, p.156.
59. 'Abdu'l-Bahá, *Paris Talks*, p.72.
60. W. Heitler, *Der Mensch und die naturwissenschaftliche Erkenntnis*, p.45. Friedrich Vieweg & Sohn, Braunschweig.
61. 'Abdu'l-Bahá, *Paris Talks*, p.25.